RAINBOW
CUISINE

LANNICE SNYMAN

Photography by
ANDRZEJ SAWA

RAINBOW
CUISINE

LANNICE SNYMAN

Photography by ANDRZEJ SAWA

KÖNEMANN

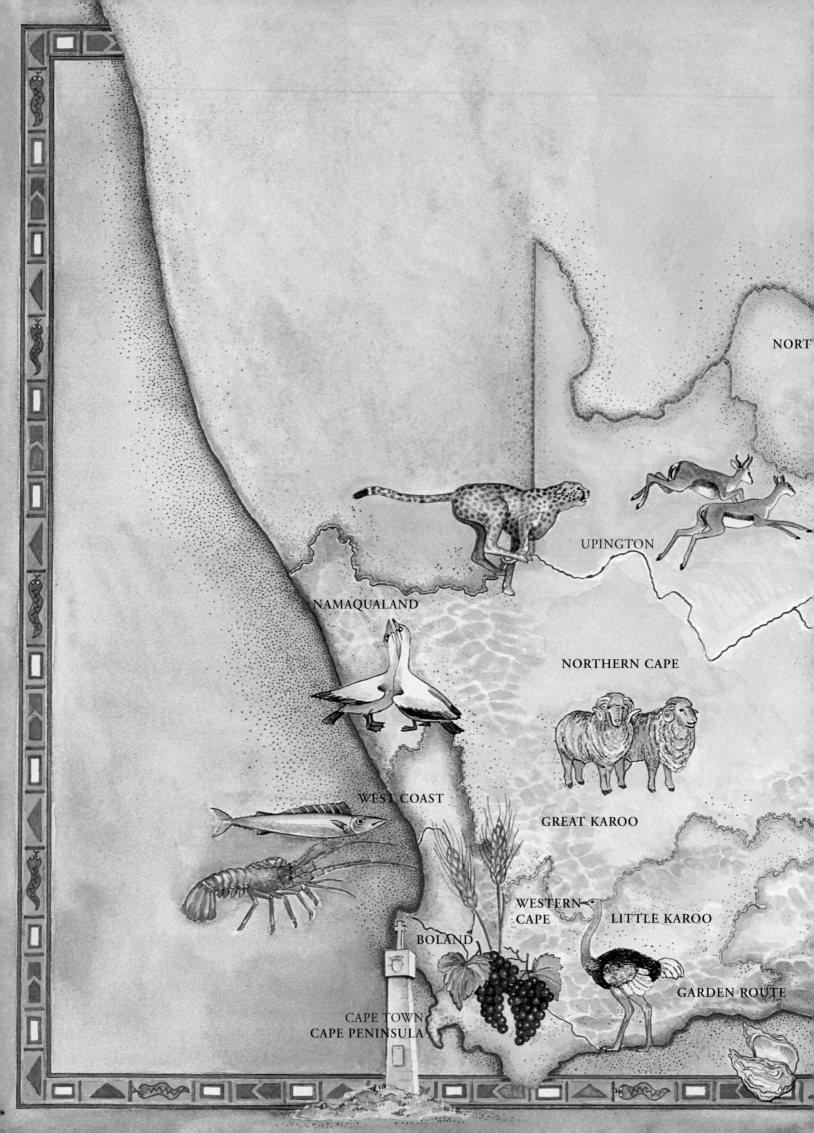

NORT

UPINGTON

NAMAQUALAND

NORTHERN CAPE

WEST COAST

GREAT KAROO

WESTERN
CAPE

LITTLE KAROO

BOLAND

GARDEN ROUTE

CAPE TOWN
CAPE PENINSULA

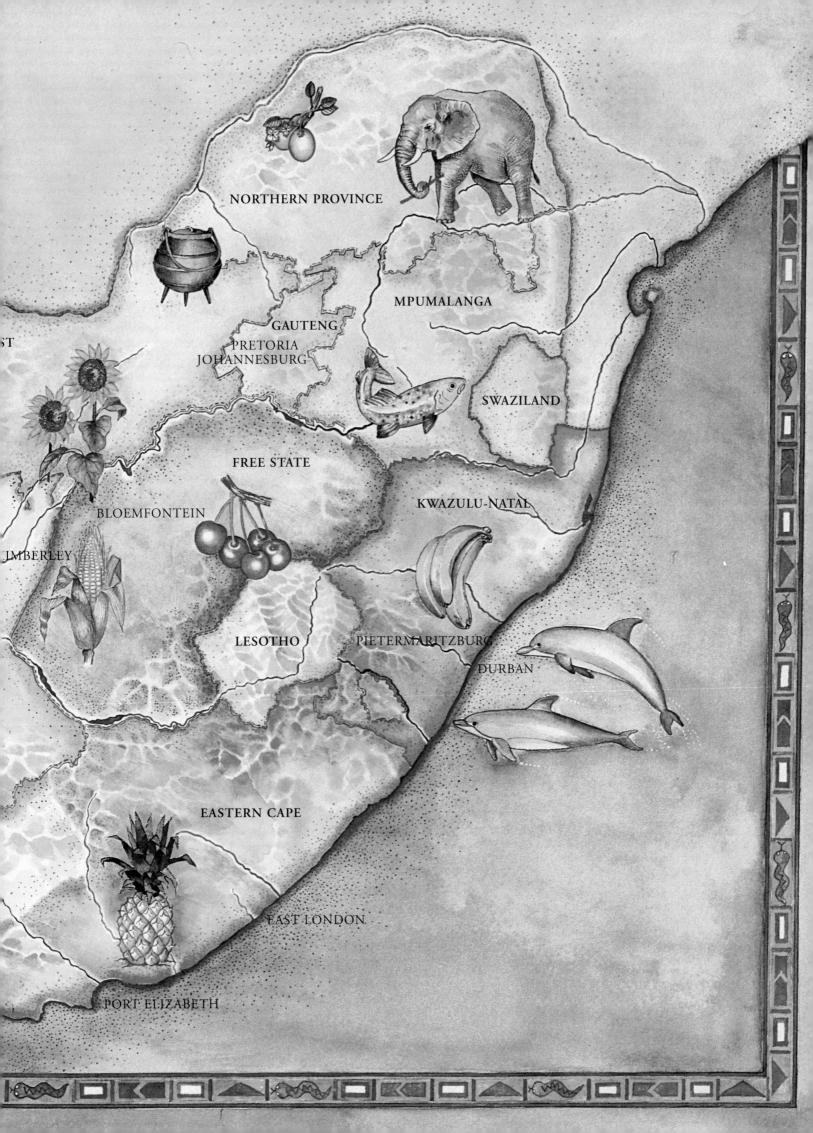

DEDICATION

Practised hands pattern a bowl of pap (maize-meal porridge) with a dried corn cob. The simple scene on the cover
is played out in South Africa in a myriad ways, and with countless different dishes, encompassing everything
that is good about food – respect for ingredients, cooking skills, and careful presentation.

Rainbow Cuisine is not only dedicated to all those who cooked for us in their own special way during the years it took
to put the book together, but also the unseen hands that went before. More importantly, it is dedicated to those who,
in the future, will look back and remember how it used to be – and strive to keep the country's culinary legacy alive.

ACKNOWLEDGEMENTS

The generosity and special skills of many people are incorporated in this book. In particular:

Hotels, guest houses, country lodges, private game reserves and restaurants that hosted us while we tracked down
traditional and regional recipes. Also, the farms which provided information. They are listed on page 221.

South African Airways and Nissan South Africa, for providing us with transport during the early years of research.

The Bureau and, in particular, Alfred Obendorfer and Gunter Grumptman, for the reproduction of our photographs.

ISO Photo for sponsoring the Fuji Film.

Fotoquip, stockists of Hasselblad cameras – used exclusively for the food photography – for their assistance in
obtaining the Broncolor lighting system.

Dennis Barling, for the loan of original paintings for the photographs, and Lynette Barling, for editing the text.

Volker Miros, who took the photograph of us for the jacket.

Most importantly, to our wonderful and patient families – Dana Sawa, and Michael, Courtenay and Tamsin Snyman –
who seldom complained as they watched us setting off on yet another journey along untravelled paths.

We trust it was all worth it!

AUTHOR AND STYLIST Lannice Snyman
PHOTOGRAPHER Andrzej Sawa FRPS FPSSA FPPSA
DESIGN Ninety Six Inc.
STUDIO FOOD STYLING ASSISTANT Tamsin Snyman
BRAAIER FOR PHOTOGRAPHY Michael Snyman
CREATIVE EDITOR Lynette Barling
COPY EDITOR Brenda Brickman
MAP Georgina Steyn

CONTENTS

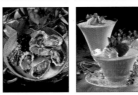

INTRODUCTION

THE POUNDING OF WOODEN pestles in time-worn mortars; the grinding of aged stone against stone; the sizzle of meat over the coals of an open fire; the crack of shellfish being prised opened; the bubbling of a potjie – these were the sounds of early South African cooking.

Much has changed in three hundred years; much remains the same. While we observe the inevitable demise of some age-old practises and cooking skills, we take pride as South African culinary art enters the spotlight of the world's food stage, and watch as it makes its mark as an internationally-acclaimed cuisine.

It has been our privilege and pleasure to undertake a culinary journey of discovery to bring together, for the first time, South Africa's rich and varied menus, and to explore the historical and regional culinary idiosyncrasies of a vast and varied country.

Recipes, however, have little value when divorced from the folk who cook them, or from the bountiful land that provides the ingredients. By setting the food against the beauty of South

Africa's scenic splendour, *Rainbow Cuisine* maintains this synergy.

Considering the enormity of the task of the research and photography, and taking into account the diverse origins, lifestyles, colours, preferences and aspirations of our people, it is little wonder that *Rainbow Cuisine* took so many years to put together, and involved thousands of kilometres of travelling to accessible (and some seemingly inaccessible) parts of the country.

Yet we did not work alone, as the wonderful thing about food is the fact that eating means sharing, whether it be a humble snack, a casual campfire repast, a gourmet meal or a banquet unifying people of every race, colour or creed. And coming together in this way is one of the most powerful and intimate forms of communication there is.

We shared this intimacy with many folk who afforded us hospitality and cooked for us in their traditional way. Bushmen in the Cape hills who still hunt with bows and arrows; VhaVenda people in the Northern Province who introduced us to plump mopane worms and multi-tiered king's porridge; Xhosa women in the Eastern Cape who baked potbrood in the coals of their fire, and simmered samp and beans in a three-legged potjie; colourful Ndebele people north of Gauteng who offered us freshly gathered wild greens called morogo, and a dish of mealies and pumpkin; Zulus in KwaZulu-Natal who prepared beef stew with dumplings, and nutritious madumbe roots; West Coast fisherfolk with whom we shared seafood prepared in many different ways.

In contrast, cooks in private homes, and chefs at restaurants, hotels, guest houses and game lodges prepared dishes using the best foods of their region – plump trout from the streams of the Eastern Highlands, herb-sweet lamb, and porridge prepared with stone-ground meal in the dusty Karoo, blesbok in the heart of the Free State, black mussels on a West Coast beach, rock lobster in the Cape peninsula, ostrich in Oudtshoorn, oysters in Knysna, wild birds and sub-tropical fruit in the KwaZulu-Natal Midlands, and tender venison in 'big game country'.

To all who have opened their hearts and homes, and shared with us their culinary vision and wisdom – as well as their recipes – we are deeply indebted.

As elsewhere in the world, the South African table has been forged by a vital force that spurs man on to borrow from his past, take into account the present, yet look to the future.

South African cuisine is many things to many people, and books have been written on 'boerekos', Cape-Malay cooking, Indian cuisine, Portuguese fare, black African foods and suchlike. Each, until now, has been treated as a separate entity, and has largely ignored the way these people and their recipes intertwined. Furthermore, the few international cookbooks published on African food tend to bypass entirely the cuisine of South Africa. *Rainbow Cuisine* eloquently puts together the pieces of the puzzle.

The fare that typifies us best is Cape-Dutch Malay – shortened to Cape Cuisine – whose foundations nod to ancient Greek and Roman civilisations which, through the passage of many centuries, were altered, elaborated on, and improved by European cooks of originality and ingenuity.

The special local fillips which set South African cuisine apart, though, are indigenous African tribal cooking, as well as a generous soupçon of spicing introduced by slaves and indentured labourers from eastern lands.

Subsequently the food heritage of others – French, German, British, Scottish, Italian, Greek, Portuguese, Mauritian, Chinese, Jewish and Indian among them – have impacted on our menus, and added to our list of recipes.

All these influences are to be found in the recipes in this book. Many stem from gems discovered in the pages of our earliest cookbooks, themselves adaptations of European recipes – most requiring a dash of innovation to bring them up-to-date. Some indicate a merging of ideas; others remain true to their origins. Many are rooted in the mists of time while several have been influenced by the modern kitchen. A few are new innovations from a country with a strong regional pride.

Rainbow Cuisine: A Culinary Journey through South Africa, therefore, is a joyous celebration of South Africa, its people and its cuisine.

Enjoy!

Lannice Snyman   Andrzej Sawa

CHAPTER ONE

THE PEOPLE OF SOUTH AFRICA

CULINARY HERITAGE OF A RAINBOW NATION

A KALEIDOSCOPE OF COLOURS, creeds and social backgrounds makes up the South African nation, creating an extraordinarily complex society and a patchwork of food styles, lifestyles and cuisines.

Some of the country's people have dwelt here since the mists of time; many have immigrated from far-flung corners of the globe. This diversity might seem good reason for a fragmented nation, yet to know this land and its people is to know how inexplicably unified the nation is, and how deeply their roots are buried in African soil.

South Africa's place in the larger global village has been wrought by the tenacity of hunter-gatherers, migratory pastoralists, and pioneers, to survive in a troubled political and social arena, and a harsh, unforgiving terrain. Though the country has only recently begun to make inroads in the world's better-established and more famous cuisines, it was probably in Africa that Man began, and where he mastered the art of fire-making – without which cooking and survival would have been improbable.

Copper-coloured San (known as Bushmen), South Africa's oldest residents and ardent lovers of freedom, are true children of nature. With an innate understanding of their environment, they have lived off land and sea since the Stone Age, subsisting in areas which, due to the advance of both whites and blacks, continue to shrink in size. The few remaining scatterlings of this ancient tribe cling to their past

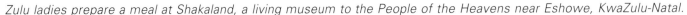

Zulu ladies prepare a meal at Shakaland, a living museum to the People of the Heavens near Eshowe, KwaZulu-Natal.

A San (Bushman) father shares some quality time with his baby at Kagga Kamma, deep in the Koue Bokkeveld.

A member of the Tembe Thonga tribe prepares to spear a fish in Lake Sifungu near Kosi Bay in KwaZulu-Natal.

with an ever-decreasing degree of success. Few men now hunt with bows and arrows, their tips dipped in poison; few women still gather plant food from the barren desert, scrub and fynbos – skills at which their forebears were incredibly adept, and which are sadly dying out.

The Khoi, or Khoikhoi (whom European settlers called Hottentots) were also initially hunter-gatherers. They learned the art of herding cattle and fat-tailed sheep, formed a loose society with the San, and lived in the rich grazing lands of the southern Cape coastal regions. However, their wandering lifestyle and lack of hereditary chieftainship created a fragile social infrastructure. Settler expansion, drought, disease and livestock theft took their toll. Traditional ways of life died out, and eventually their society was absorbed into the rest of the population.

Anthropologists coined the name Khoisan as a term to embrace the San and Khoi, who were of common stock.

The unhurried path of black pastoralists, who ventured south from the Congo basin in the region of the Great Lakes of central East Africa, took several centuries, a journey governed by geographic, social and political dictates. Tribes split in several directions, some remaining in the interior, others filtering down the east coast. Despite shared roots, clans developed in isolation, and formed several broad ethnic groups, each retaining its own cultural identity, language and traditional ways of cooking. They finally came into contact and conflict with the Khoisan, with each other and, inevitably, with Europeans on their own treks from the Cape colony into the hinterland.

What little is known of the way of life of early African man has been gleaned from various sources, including word of mouth, ancient middens, and the rock art of the San, who painted on walls of caves in such diverse locations as the Cape Peninsula, Zimbabwe, Swaziland and Namibia.

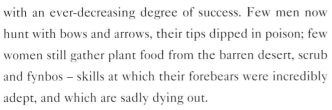

THE PEOPLE OF SOUTH AFRICA

Snippets of information stem from the writings of Portuguese sailors, frequent callers at the Cape's coast during the sixteenth century while on voyages of discovery – quests spurred on by trade and the search for gold, precious stones, ivory, amber and spices. They told of Strandlopers (also called Watermen, outcasts from the Khoikhoi community), who built stone traps to ensnare fish as the tide receded, and collected seafood. They also described the lifestyle of black hunters, herders and cultivators, telling of rich pastures, and of success in tilling and planting.

They wrote of millet (indigenous to Africa and Asia), 'white and the size of peppercorns', being pounded into flour between stones or in wooden mortars with pestles, and of the flour being made into cakes and baked in the embers of fires. They described how millet was fermented for beer, much the way it is still made today, and how it was strained through birds nests. Mention was made of crops such as melons, beans, gourds and sugar cane (more likely a variety of sorghum) known as 'sweet cane'.

This then was the primitive culinary inheritance of Jan van Riebeeck, who was sent to Africa's southernmost tip by the Dutch East India Company in 1652 to establish a refreshment station for ships plying the sea route between West and East. He found a lifestyle embedded in a land and people to whom food was a matter of survival, rather than an art to elevate to a higher creative form.

The new South Africans quickly learned skills from indigenous peoples who had already mastered the art of survival. They bartered for sustenance, learnt to hunt and fish, gathered wild plants for food and for medicinal purposes, including as a treatment for scurvy. From these humble, shared foundations grew a fascinating, extraordinarily complex cuisine.

TOP *Xhosa women performing a traditional dance near Bathurst in the Eastern Cape.*
CENTRE *VhaVenda women in traditional garb make a cooking fire in the old-fashioned way. Venda, a former 'homeland', is now incorporated in Northern Province.*
LEFT *Throughout history, Ndebele people have adorned themselves, and their houses, with bright colours.*

14

Cape Malay chef, Achmat Marcus and his wife Faldeelah, host a feast for family and friends.

Holland ruled the Cape of Good Hope for some 150 years, during which time European elements were added to indigenous African cuisine. Accomplished cooks, the Dutch were influenced by their colonies which had easy access to ingredients such as rice, and gentle spices like nutmeg and cinnamon. Their fondness for vegetables, fish and lavish quantities of butter (or fat) added richness and a certain stodginess that still distinguishes Cape-Dutch recipes.

From as early as 1667, Malay slaves and political exiles were brought from Java and other Indonesian islands. They were fine artisans, fishermen, seamstresses, tailors and basket-makers – and excellent cooks – whose skills were eagerly sought after and appreciated by their European masters.

By refining what was already in place, adding Eastern nuances, and making excellent use of local ingredients from land and sea, their impact on the Cape table was profound. Their unique cooking skills were eloquently summed up by C Louis Leipoldt, in his book *Leipoldt's Cape Cookery*: 'Their outstanding characteristics are the free, almost heroic, use of spices and aromatic flavourings, the prolonged, steady but slow application of moist heat to meat dishes, and the skilful blending of many diverse constituents into a combination that still holds the essential goodness of each.'

Like women throughout history who have moved to strange lands, Malays brought with them spices to remind them of home. These, including their multi-flavoured

Joe Harry displays a bright array of Indian spices at his shop, Joe's Corner Shop, in Durban's Victoria Street market.

masalas, added exotic flavour to Cape dishes. Spicy sambals, chutneys and pickles added interest and fired up palates more familiar with bland European fare. They introduced the pleasure of combining sweet and sour, a significant characteristic of South African cooking.

Despite intermarriage between all the races at the Cape – which resulted in the Cape coloured population – the Cape Malays maintained their Muslim faith and their community has remained a distinct entity. They uphold and respect their culture and traditions, and, though merging naturally with Dutch, Indian, English and French influences, their recipes still remain true to those of their forebears.

French cultural and culinary finesse was introduced between 1688 and 1690, with the arrival of a small group of French Huguenots – Protestant refugees in search of religious freedom. At that time the free population of the colony numbered only about 600 burghers. The Huguenots influenced our cuisine, specifically through their appreciation of fruit and skills with by-products such as raisins and confitures (jams and preserves which we call konfyt). More importantly, though, we laud them for the success of our wine industry, for they were selected specifically for their competence in 'cultivating the vine', settling along the Berg River, in Drakenstein and De Olifantshoek, which, in time, became known as Franschhoek. The entire region would later be known as the Cape winelands, where still today many villages, streets and towns are named after their original French founders.

In the late 1700s Britain assumed rulership of the Cape and introduced a distinctive colonial lifestyle. French and Danish ships called at Table Bay, as did vessels from other European ports and from the United States of America.

Yet another significant event, in human terms, occurred in 1820 with an influx of British settlers brought here to augment the white population in the troubled eastern frontier region. They have become a symbol of British contribution to our society, culture and cuisine, especially in introducing pies, hot puddings and roast meats to our recipe repertoire.

An immigration plan some thirty years later added yet another dimension to an already multi-cultural land – the resettling of German peasants and soldiers of the disbanded Anglo-German Legion who had fought against Russia in the Crimean War. Many later relocated to what is now Namibia, but some chose to remain in South Africa. German influence is present in many of our dishes, especially their predilection for wurst (sausage) and hearty casseroles, and their deft handling of meat and potatoes.

Threads of the tapestry of South Africa's cuisine continued to be woven together. Indians were brought as indentured labourers to the coastlands of Natal in the mid-1800s to work on sugar farms. Many stayed on after their contracts expired, and Indian dishes – notably curries – became an integral part of our menu. Initially ingredients were imported; later the settlement grew its own rice, chillies, ginger, cumin, coriander and garlic, but continued to bring tamarind, black pepper, mace, nutmeg, saffron and coconut from the East.

The discovery of gold along the Witwatersrand in the Transvaal Republic in 1886 attracted not only investment from Britain, America and Germany, but also mineworkers, businessmen and professionals from these countries, as well as from Australia and eastern Europe. In the ensuing years more and more people became attracted to the sunny South African lifestyle, enriching us with their own knowledge, culture and culinary traditions.

As for present trends and future predictions of South African cooking, the story continues to unfold. With urbanisation, the dismantling of the apartheid system and the upsurgance of interracial harmony, has come a re-evaluation of long-fragmented traditions. Urban black people have adopted aspects of Western diet, which has led to the demise of indigenous ingredients, traditional dishes and cooking methods. Frying, for example, has usurped the time-honoured roasting of meat; maize meal is generally bought in packets and no longer ground between two stones; and the younger generation seldom asks its elders for advice on the foods of times gone by!

Farmer Hannes Saaiman mans his fresh vegetable stall – on the back of his bakkie at the Bainsvlei Farmers' Market near Bloemfontein, Free State.

On the other hand, whites are looking to their roots with renewed interest and embracing more and more the ingredients, recipes and cooking techniques favoured by black communities. Dishes like pap (maize-meal porridge), samp and beans, mopane worms and morogo are crossing the black/white divide. Home cooks, food writers and restaurateurs are rethinking their inherited culinary ethic and merging our myriad styles into a harmonious, yet multi-faceted, whole.

Those who visit our shores, enjoy our special hospitality, dine in our restaurants and follow our recipes will find much on the South African table that bears testimony to all who comprise the complex rainbow of South African people.

CHAPTER TWO
BREAKFAST

A SOUTH AFRICAN BREAKFAST may be as simple as a rusk dunked into a mug of coffee, as homely as a bowl of porridge, or as healthy as juicy, sun-ripened fruit – for which the country is justly famous – or fruit salad. Often, though, families tuck into a hearty cooked breakfast of eggs, bacon, tomato, mushrooms and sausage, sometimes with chops, steak, kidneys and liver too.

Prior to the cultivation of cereals, breakfast in rural black homes consisted simply of nutritious amasi (curdled milk). With cereal crops came the widespread popularity of porridge, either mixed with amasi, or splashed with milk or cream and sweet-ened with honey. Though made from a wide variety of grains, including sorghum and millet, maize meal is the most popular. Mealies were brought from America. Rural cooking is still done, as in days long gone, in clay pots over open fires, while practised hands twirl stirring sticks to an ancient rhythm, eloquently display-ing the skills employed in tradition-al cooking. For example VhaVenda women in the far north ladle mukonde (king's porridge) onto a flat wooden dish. The many layers form a pyramid as they set. Many societies demonstrate the affection a woman has for her husband by intricately patterning his porridge with a corn cob.

Our breakfasts have become more cosmopolitan in recent times, yet traditional dishes like frikkadelle, sosaties and skilpadjies (liver wrapped in caul fat) often pop up on morn-ing menus. At coastal venues you may be offered fresh oys-ters, black mussels, fish cakes, smoorsnoek and poached haddock. In trout-farming areas fresh or smoked trout is

OPPOSITE *A heavily bangled Ndebele woman grinds maize into meal between two stones.*
ABOVE *Breakfast buffet at Carrigans Country Estate in Mpumalanga: fresh fruit, bread, Honey-Toasted Muesli (page 22) and Green Fig Preserve (page 173).*

always on the menu. Regional recipes are particularly delightful, like the Hantam speciality of stone-ground boermeel (farmer's meal) porridge studded with raisins which, in days past were bartered from travelling Jewish peddlers. Kambrokonfyt (kambro jam) – made from the roots of potato-like tubers – is a local treat, and is delicious on toast.

The special thing about African mornings is the wonderful weather. Breakfast is served outdoors on urban stoeps and rural patios, in sandy coves and leafy country gardens – not to mention in dry river beds snaking through private game reserves, where breakfast is a welcome break in a morning game drive with untamed bushveld all around.

 A typical south african breakfast: eggs, bacon, tomatoes and boerewors, with toast and butter.

MAIZE-MEAL PORRIDGE

Pap (porridge) has been prepared through the centuries,
varying in texture from stiff and crumbly to thin and runny.
Though pre-packaging has caused the demise of the time-honoured
art of grinding meal by hand between two stones, purists still
maintain that the tastiest porridge is made from hand-ground
meal. Slow, steady heat is important, as is the stirring stick
(precursor of the ubiquitous wooden spoon), which takes different
forms in different societies. This is the 'Boland' way of
preparing maize-meal porridge.

500 ml maize meal
5 ml salt
1,5 litres water
30 g (30 ml) butter

Mix the maize meal and salt into 500 ml of the water. Bring
the remainder to the boil in a large, heavy pot and add the
maize meal mixture little by little, stirring constantly. Cover,
reduce the heat and simmer very gently for 15 minutes, stirring occasionally. Mix in the butter and serve hot with milk
or cream, and runny honey or sugar.
SERVES 8

STYWEPAP (Gauteng's favourite – most often served at a
braai with fresh tomato sauce!) Bring 1 litre water and 5 ml
salt to the boil in a large, heavy pot. Tip in 500 ml maize
meal all in one go, mix quickly, cover and cook undisturbed
over very gentle heat for about 15 minutes. Mix in 30 g
(30 ml) butter and serve hot.
SERVES 8

KRUMMELPAP Also called putupap, is the favourite of
Free Staters and Zulu folk, who serve it with amasi (curdled
milk) for breakfast, or as a main meal, with vegetables, or
dipped into the gravy of a meat stew. Bring 1 litre water and
5 ml salt to the boil in a large, heavy pot. Tip in 750 ml maize
meal, stirring constantly. Cover and cook over very low heat
for about 15 minutes, stirring every 5 minutes to keep the
mixture loose and crumbly. Mix in 30 g (30 ml) butter just
before serving.
SERVES 8

MAIZE-RICE
AND SORGHUM PORRIDGE

Based on a favourite of the Swazi and Tswana
people. Malt-flavoured sorghum meal or grain sorghum (amabele
or mabele in most black languages) is mixed with maize rice –
crushed, dried corn kernels – and cooked with milk.

125 ml maize rice
125 ml sorghum meal (Maltabella)
250 ml water
500 ml milk
2 ml salt

Measure maize rice into a bowl, add cold water to cover
generously and set aside for at least 8 hours. Drain well.

Mix together the sorghum meal and water. Bring the milk
and salt to the boil in a pot, add the drained maize rice and
simmer, uncovered, for 5 minutes, stirring occasionally. Stir
in the sorghum mixture and cook for 15 minutes more, stirring occasionally. Serve with milk and honey.
SERVES 4

HONEY-TOASTED MUESLI

*Muesli, a Swiss creation, has become everyone's favourite
healthy breakfast. Substitute almonds with other nuts, and add
whatever dried fruit you fancy. Store in an airtight
container in the fridge.*

500 ml oats
250 ml bran
250 ml desiccated coconut
125 ml wheat germ
125 ml sesame seeds
125 ml sunflower seeds
100 g flaked or slivered almonds
60 ml vegetable oil
125 ml runny honey
250 ml sultanas or seedless raisins

Set the oven at 140°C. Toss the oats, bran, coconut, wheat
germ, sesame seeds, sunflower seeds and almonds evenly in
a large roasting dish.

Mix together the oil and honey in a small saucepan and
heat gently until the mixture is nice and runny. Pour over
the muesli and mix in gently.

Bake uncovered for about 60 minutes until golden, stirring
every 10 minutes or so.

Allow to cool and add the sultanas or raisins. Serve with
plain yoghurt and honey.

MAKES ABOUT 1,7 LITRES

COMPOTE OF DRIED FRUIT

*Dried fruit, produced prolifically in the western
and northern regions of the Cape, finds its way
into many dishes, both sweet and savoury.*

500 g mixed dried fruit
1 litre freshly squeezed orange juice
grated rind and juice of 1 lemon
15 ml brown sugar
2 cinnamon sticks
4 whole cloves

*A breakfast tray with Compote of Dried Fruit, Bran
Muffins with Raisins (page 209), and coffee.*

Combine the dried fruit, orange juice, lemon rind and juice,
brown sugar, cinnamon and cloves in a saucepan. Cover and
simmer for 5 minutes. Remove from the heat and set aside
for a couple of hours for the fruit to plump. Transfer to a
glass serving bowl, cover and chill in the fridge, where it
may be stored for up to 5 days.

SERVES 8-10

KEDGEREE

This spicy dish emanates from India, but Victorian England popularised it and introduced it to Africa. Chilli, ginger and turmeric are called for in this version; omit them for a more 'English' flavour.

500 ml water
1 bunch fresh herbs
(bay leaf, parsley sprig, fennel frond)
4 black peppercorns
400 g haddock (smoked hake)
1 large onion, chopped
80 g butter
5 ml curry powder
5 ml salt
milled black pepper
2 ml turmeric
2-3 thin slices green ginger
1 small red or green chilli, sliced and seeded
250 ml uncooked rice
60 ml cream
lemon juice
4 hard-boiled eggs, shelled and quartered

Bring the water to the boil in a wide saucepan with the bunch of herbs and the peppercorns. Add the haddock, cover and poach very slowly (the liquid should barely move) until cooked. Thin fillets will take about 6 minutes; plumper steaks require a few minutes longer.

Drain fish, remove and discard skin (this is easiest to do while it's still hot). Flake the flesh and set aside. Strain the poaching liquid into a measuring jug and make up to 500 ml with boiling water.

In a saucepan fry the onion in butter until golden. Add the curry powder, salt, pepper, turmeric, ginger and chilli and stir for about 30 seconds to sizzle the spices. Stir in the rice, then add the poaching liquid. Cover and simmer gently until the liquid has been absorbed and the rice is cooked. Stir in haddock and cream, flavour with lemon juice, and heat through.

Pile kedgeree onto a hot serving dish and garnish with quartered, hard-boiled eggs.

SERVES 6-8

FISH WITH EGGS SCRAMBLE

Here's a delicious olden-day omelette that incorporates the intriguing spirit of Cape-Malay flavouring. Egg dishes were extraordinarily popular in early Cape cookery. Besides hen's eggs, penguin eggs were enjoyed, as well as eggs from ducks, peahens, turkeys, geese, ostriches, guineafowl and wild ducks. Turtle and tortoise eggs, too, were sometimes to be had. Fish omelettes (prepared with both fish and shellfish) were well known, like this unusual recipe from a late eighteenth-century manuscript. It may be prepared with any type of fish, from economical hake to luxury lines like haddock (smoked hake), smoked salmon and smoked trout.

500 g filleted, skinless fish
salt and milled black pepper
6 eggs
30 ml brandy
60 ml full-cream milk
or cream
15 ml fresh thyme leaves
1 small sprig fresh rosemary
butter, vegetable oil
1 large onion, sliced
1 ml turmeric
1 red or green chilli, sliced
and seeded

Cut the fish into small pieces, about 5-cm-square (Cape Malays call them mootjies). Season lightly with salt and pepper. Lightly whisk together the eggs, brandy and milk or cream in a jug with the thyme and rosemary.

Heat a little butter and oil in a frying pan and fry the onion until golden brown. Stir in the turmeric and chilli. Sizzle for about 30 seconds, then add the fish and fry gently until browned on all sides and almost cooked (smoked fish merely needs to be heated through).

Pour in the egg mixture and cook over very gentle heat, stirring constantly, until softly set. Discard the rosemary and serve immediately.

SERVES 3-4

TOMATO-BAKED EGGS

The English love bacon, eggs and tomato for breakfast, and this is the way British travellers in the 'outposts of the Empire' started their day whilst on safari in the wilds of Africa in the 1930s and 1940s. Besides being delicious for breakfast, it makes an interesting light supper.

6 large, ripe tomatoes
salt and milled black pepper
6 eggs, at room temperature
15 ml grape vinegar
6 rashers rindless bacon, chopped
vegetable oil
250 ml fresh white or brown breadcrumbs
30 ml chopped fresh parsley

Set the oven at 200°C. Cut a thick slice off the top of each tomato and remove pith and seeds. Season cavities with salt and pepper and set aside to drain, cut-side down.

Soft boil the eggs: prick the round end with a pin or egg pricker, place in a single layer in a saucepan, and add enough cold water to cover by 10 mm. Add the vinegar and pinch of salt. Bring to the boil; boil for 1 minute, then switch off the heat, cover the saucepan and allow to stand for 3 minutes. Plunge eggs into cold water and remove shells.

Fry the bacon until crisp in a little oil in a frying pan. Remove from the stove and mix in the crumbs and parsley. Pop an egg into each tomato, place in a baking dish and top with crumb mixture. Bake for 10-15 minutes. Serve with toast.
SERVES 6

SMOKED TROUT OMELETTE

The tranquil Eastern Highlands of Mpumalanga is where the bulk of our trout-farming is done, and travellers are assured of a feast of trout at every pub, restaurant and hotel in the area.

40 g onion, finely chopped
butter, vegetable oil
100 g skinless, filleted, smoked trout, flaked
3 eggs
45 ml water
salt, milled black pepper, paprika
100 g Emmental cheese, grated

Preheat the oven griller. Soften the onion in a little butter in a frying pan. Add the trout. Heat through and set aside.

Whisk the eggs and water with a hand whisk until frothy, and season with salt, pepper and a dash of paprika.

Heat a little more butter and oil (about 15 ml each) in an omelette pan and pour in the egg mixture. Push it away from the sides towards the centre with a spatula as it sets, and allow the runny mixture to run to the sides.

When almost cooked, place the pan under the grill so that the omelette puffs up. Scatter the trout and onion mixture and cheese over the egg mixture. Fold over in half and serve with cocktail tomatoes.
SERVES 1-2

BLACK MUSHROOMS IN SHERRY

Mushrooms once grew wild on Table Mountain, as well as on the Cape Flats, where German farmers established smallholdings in the late 1800s.

6 large black mushrooms, wiped clean
50 g butter
2-3 cloves garlic, crushed
30 ml finely shredded fresh sage leaves
milled black pepper
125 ml medium-dry sherry

Heat the butter and garlic until sizzling in frying pan large enough to hold all six mushrooms snugly. Place in the pan gills down and fry gently for 2-3 minutes. Turn, and fry for a further 1-2 minutes.

Scatter with sage, season with pepper, sprinkle with sherry, and cover with a lid large enough to seal the pan. Reduce the heat and cook gently for a few minutes until the centre stalks are tender when pierced with a skewer.

Transfer mushrooms to a warm platter. Boil the cooking liquid, uncovered, until slightly reduced. Spoon over the mushrooms, garnish with chives or shallots and serve hot.
SERVES 6

DEVILLED LAMB'S KIDNEYS

These may be prepared a day ahead and chilled, but don't add the brandy and cream until you reheat.

10-12 lamb's kidneys
juice of ½ lemon or 15 ml wine vinegar
vegetable oil, milled black pepper
250 g rindless streaky bacon, chopped
2 onions, roughly chopped
200 ml Meat Stock (page 216)
30 ml Worcestershire sauce
45 ml cake flour
125 ml water
125 ml cream
45 ml brandy

Soak the kidneys for 30 minutes in cold water to which the lemon juice or vinegar has been added. Drain, rinse and pat dry. Cut into halves and remove the skin, white core and sinews. Cut each half into 2-3 chunks.

Heat a little oil in a medium saucepan and fry the bacon until it's fairly crisp. Add the onion, stir for a minute then add the kidneys. Cook uncovered over high heat for about 10-15 minutes, stirring occasionally at first, then constantly as the moisture cooks away and the kidneys brown. Add the stock, Worcestershire sauce and pepper. Cover and simmer for about 5 minutes.

Blend the flour with a little of the hot sauce and the water in a small bowl. Stir into the pan and simmer until the sauce thickens. Add the cream and brandy and heat through. Serve on toast, or with bacon and eggs.
SERVES 8

CHAPTER THREE
CAPE PENINSULA
& BOLAND

LOBSTERS, LINEFISH AND NEW WORLD WINES

THE TIP OF AFRICA, OUR social and culinary heartland, is so different from the rest of the country as to seem entirely separate. Oceans, mountains and vineyards form an enchanting backdrop to the southern Cape lifestyle, which creates a wonderful synergy between upbeat city living and tranquil country pursuits – an enviable harmony of work and play. And on the Cape table are foods from sea and farmland, accompanied by the finest New World wines.

Changing seasons, so dramatic in this part of the world, play an important part in setting food fashions apart from other regions of the sub-continent. Spring, summer, autumn, winter - each in its own unique way – heralds new crops and different menu ideas.

Elsewhere rain falls in summer; here winter downpours soak lands that provide much of the country's fruit and vegetables.

Wild mushrooms proliferate in woodland forests when rain and sun have worked their magic; waterblommetjies may be plucked from farm dams for winter bredies; berries ripen in early summer and are piled into tarts, boiled into jam, and steeped in brandy for the coming months. Fruit like peaches, nectarines, plums, grapes, pears and apples ripen in well-tended orchards.

Unlike the landlocked provinces to the north, currents of two great oceans – the warm Mozambique of the Indian; the icy Benguela of the Atlantic – sweep past the Cape Peninsula, impacting on weather, crops and the migration of fish.

The historical Boschendal Estate in the shadow of the majestic Groot Drakenstein and Simonsberg mountains in the Cape winelands. Workers prune the famous vines in front of the manor house, which was built in 1812.

Fishermen at Kalk Bay harbour wind-dry their fish by pegging them to the rigging of their boats.

Seafoods are an integral part of Cape menus, and no-one knows more than *Kaapenaars* about the delights of fresh fish roasting over open coals, rock lobster (crayfish) simmering seductively in a pot, perlemoen (abalone) steaks sizzling in butter, and freshly gathered black mussels spilling ambrosial juices into a mix of onion, wine and herbs.

Sports fishermen try their luck for fish like geelbek, kob, red steenbras, roman, stumpnose, steenbras and the elusive galjoen – our national fish which is named after the stately Spanish sailing vessel. The summer gamefish season attracts anglers from all over the world to troll for tuna, yellowtail and marlin in the deep, azure waters off Cape Point.

Fishermen eagerly anticipate the snoek season that runs for several weeks in late winter, working hard to capitalize on the catch, in the way of their forebears. Instinct and financial reward guide their lines, as efforts to track migratory patterns of shoals have long escaped logic. Here they are braaied (grilled), smoked, pickled and made into smoorsnoek, a spicy mélange of fish and rice.

Cape Town, the Mother City, is sheltered in a natural bowl formed by the Table Mountain massif. A grand backdrop that is 1087 metres high, 150 million years old, and home to unique vegetation, Table Mountain is flanked by Devil's Peak and Lion's Head. A flagstaff was erected on the pinnacle, fires were lit, and distant West Coast farmers would watch for smoke signaling the arrival of ships – and hungry sailors – in Table Bay. They would hastily round up livestock and crops and bring them to sell at the markets.

The legendary hospitality of the Tavern of the Seas, as the city became known, started in 1652, when Jan van Riebeeck, our first 'inn keeper' grew vegetables for passing seafarers in his famous garden. Fresh drinking water was abundant, fruit and vegetable crops flourished, and soon demand outstripped supply.

Late summer sunlight floods the Hout Bay valley, with views over the bay to Kommetjie in the distance.
Alphen Hotel, set in one of the great houses of the Cape, is part of a complex of buildings set in sixteen hectares of parkland in the Constantia valley. The estate has been in the Cloete family since 1850.

A profusion of wild herbs flavoured early Cape dishes, and, in days gone by, bunches of aromatic leaves were hung up to dry from the reeded ceilings of farmhouses. Leaves of lemon and peach trees imparted their own special flavour, and are still used today by nostalgic cooks. Non-indigenous, dried spices were brought from the East, and salt was collected from the pans in Salt River.

After slaves were brought from Java and neighbouring Indonesian islands, Malay eating houses appeared on the scene, attracting portly burghers, passing seamen, and soldiers of the garrison, who thoroughly enjoyed tucking into inexpensive meals redolent of spicy eastern cuisines. Now, as then, Cape Malays are considered great hosts, for whom religious and family feasts are a way of life.

Many still reside in the architecturally and socially unique Bokaap, also called the Malay Quarter, on the slopes of Signal Hill on the city's fringe. The area has been declared a national monument, and picturesque streets are lined with beautifully maintained dwellings, which formerly housed slaves. Many are still owned by descendants of the original inhabitants for whom the houses were built.

Though early wine-making endeavours were charged more by enthusiasm than expertise, vines were imported and the Cape's oldest industry flourished in Constantia's historical farms – Groot Constantia, Klein Constantia, Bergvliet, Hoop van Constantia, Buitenverwachting, Alphen and Constantia Uitsig.

The Cape's first success was a fortified wine which emulated the fashionable tipple of Holland and England. Soon 'sweet, luscious and excellent wines' were being snaffled up and imbibed by Europe's royalty, as well as the upper crust of its society, and travellers flocked to the Cape to experience them first hand. During the halcyon days of the nineteenth century, the lush Constantia valley was the social centre of the colony, and high society life consisted of picnics, luncheons and all-day shooting parties.

Following the tracks of antelope on their seasonal migrations, settlers – followed by Voortrekkers – ventured inland through spectacular mountain passes, where rocks still bear the scars of ox wagons' wheels. By the end of the century the Boland was flourishing, our famous Cape winelands had been planted, and charming towns like Stellenbosch, Franschhoek, Paarl and Drakenstein were established.

Today these verdant winelands attract international visitors to wine, dine and relax in glorious surroundings.

31

ABOVE *A vegetable seller amongst the freshest fare at the Salt River market.*
ABOVE RIGHT *A fish vendor in Hout Bay harbour displays freshly caught snoek.*
OPPOSITE TOP *Rehana Williams holds her brightest bunches of flowers at her stall in Adderley Street.*
OPPOSITE BOTTOM *Worshippers leave the Chiappini Street mosque in the Bokaap.*

Gourmet restaurants, sophisticated hotels, charming auberges and guest houses, and homely inns are imbued with a sense of gracious living. Menus boast the freshest local produce from fish and vegetable markets; winelists include acclaimed local wines, as well as labels from other New World producers, and classics from European estates.

Like harbours around the world, Table Bay, as well as the bay at Simon's Town – previously known as Yzelstein Bay –

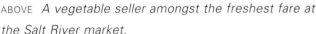

has many fascinating stories to tell about the panorama of vessels driven by sail, paddle, screw and steam, which found shelter in its protective embrace: brigs and schooners berthed with bags of coffee from Brazil, and sugar and spices from the East; ships set sail for tropical seas and southern ice floes, and for naval expeditions and maritime wars off the coast. Less illustrious visitors included convict ships and whalers en route to southern whaling grounds in search of leviathans of the deep to satisfy the world's need for soap, margarine and oil.

These same docks welcomed entrepreneurs who arrived in droves from all parts of the globe after gold and diamonds were discovered in the interior; bade farewell to soldiers during two world wars – and welcomed them home. Today, Table Bay hosts luxurious ocean liners, sleek sailing ships and racey yachts from many far-flung ports.

The area has been transformed into the Victoria & Alfred Waterfront, a development of huge historical and commercial significance, encompassing a bustling working harbour

as well as meticulously restored buildings predating the turn of the century. Restaurants and luxury hotels abound, the never-ceasing kaleidoscope of boats, barges and swooping, shrieking seabirds echoing the scene that has welcomed seafarers for more than three centuries.

The pleasures of Cape cuisine have spread to the rest of the country, although *Kaapenaars* insist that it is best enjoyed here where it began, close to its roots and the sights and sounds of the folk who empowered it and made it great.

In terms of food, fun and hospitality the Tavern of the Seas has come a long way in a very short while. Although early Malay 'cook-shops' are but a fond memory, a myriad restaurants have taken their place – some still emphasising local cuisine, many owned, managed and cheffed by fascinating folk from near and far, whose expertise has broadened our culinary scope even more.

Dining out – or dining in – the Cape peninsula and Boland certainly provides the gourmet with a world of food on one many-flavoured multi-national plate.

33

CHAPTER FOUR
SNACKS, STARTERS & SOUPS

SOUTH AFRICANS ENJOY SIMPLE snacks and starters, and unsophisticated soups. Rather than spend time preparing complicated meals, we would much rather pick at a bokkem, or plump dried mopane worms in a pot of simmering water. Snacking on a few slices of biltong is as enjoyable a treat today as it was to early trek-farmers who spiced and dried meat and nibbled it to allay the hunger pangs of a nomadic, unsettled lifestyle.

Seashore dwellers – like Strandlopers of yore – eat just as casually. What could be nicer than gathering wild oysters from the rocks, pickling a jar of periwinkles, or steaming freshly gathered black mussels over the embers of a fire, and dipping them in hot garlic butter?

When it comes to soup – undoubtedly the favourite way of starting a meal – these are a mélange of fresh ingredients at hand, and seldom studiously composed creations that require weighing, measuring and clarifying to get them just right. Rich, sustaining and gloriously flavoured – attesting to the skill of the cook rather than the author of the recipe, soups are sometimes thin, though more often substantial – harking back to times when they were thickened with mashed vegetables, tapioca, flour, rice, or egg mixed with a little wine or cream.

Traditional flavourings include a dash of curry powder or grated nutmeg, and colouring comes from saffron or turmeric. In the olden days various leaves such as beetroot,

LEFT *Pumpkin Soup (page 47) photographed in the original kitchen at Onze Rust near Bloemfontein. The farm was bought by South African President Marthinus Steyn in 1897. His descendants still live in the magnificent farmhouse, which contains a treasure trove of Free State memorabilia.*
ABOVE *Olive Spread (page 41), a regional speciality served at Dennehof Karoo Guest House in Prince Albert.*

35

spinach, and figs were favoured for this purpose. For extra flavour and nourishment, seafood soups were often augmented with a handful of fresh, green seaweed.

Home-made stock sometimes forms the base; more often the broth is formed by the patient simmering of meat, fish, vegetables and pulses. Popular adjuncts include kluitjies (dumplings), snysels (noodles), shredded bokkems for extra spiciness, and bits of bread fried in fat or oil for crunch. Plain or spiced rice may be served as an accompaniment.

Despite modern trends, and rising stars like carpaccio, smoked salmon, fancy salads and suchlike, comfort-zone recipes live on in our homes and restaurants.

Biltong (page 37), photographed at The Artists' Colony, a guest house and restaurant in Smithfield, Free State.

BILTONG

*Our all-time favourite snack – salty, spicy, dried meat –
also makes a great garnish for salads, soups and vegetables when
finely shaved with a sharp knife. Creative cooks even blend it into
pâté to spread on toast. Drying meat and fish was a necessary
method of preservation prior to refrigeration.*

*The concept isn't the sole preserve of Afrikaners, though.
An earlier delicacy – tassal meat – was similarly prepared: strips
of meat were rubbed with salt and coriander, laid in vinegar for a
time, then panfried. In rural communities, black tribes would cut
up and dry the flesh of animals that died accidentally or of
natural causes (cattle were seldom slaughtered for food).
The Swazi people call it umcweba or umcwayiba.
Coriander seeds, formerly brought from Asia, are an essential
ingredient in the preparation of good biltong. The name is Greek
for bedbugs – nasty goggas that the seeds resemble!*

2,5 kg lean meat
(venison, beef or ostrich)
60 ml coriander seeds
60 ml salt
15 ml milled black pepper

Cut the meat into strips about 2 cm x 3 cm. Roast the coriander seeds in a dry frying pan to bring out the flavour. Crush lightly with a pestle and mortar and mix with the salt and pepper. Sprinkle a little into a glass dish, top with a layer of meat strips, and season once more. Continue in this way until meat and seasoning are used up.

Refrigerate for a day, mixing every couple of hours so that the meat flavours evenly.

Hang up to dry in a suitable spot (high in the garage rafters or behind the fridge where there is some movement of air). Straightened paper-clips make handy fasteners!

Drying time is about 5 days, depending on the weather, and whether you prefer your biltong crisp or slightly moist.

*Roasted Mopane Worms. In the Northern Province,
VhaVenda women simmer dried worms in a potjie
over the fire to plump them before roasting.*

ROASTED MOPANE WORMS

*This tasty, nutritious diet staple of rural black tribes is becoming
scarcer and scarcer, and women travel long distances – even into
Botswana – to collect worms from mopane trees. The worms are
then dried and taken home as food for the family, or to be sold at
informal markets, where the purchasing measure is a tin mug!
More recently mopane worms have appeared on menus of city
restaurants, done up in some or other guise. This, though,
is a traditional way of preparation which accentuates both
flavour and texture.*

500 g dried mopane worms
salt
60 ml vegetable oil

Preheat the oven griller. Wash the worms by rubbing gently between your hands under cold, running water. Place in a pot, add sufficient water to cover and season with salt. Simmer uncovered for about 10 minutes until all the water has been absorbed and the worms are plump.

Add the oil and sizzle over high heat for about 5 minutes. Scatter the worms on a baking tray and grill for 10-15 minutes until tender and slightly crisp. Serve at room temperature.
SERVES 12 AS SNACKS

37

Bokkems hang behind a plate of fresh harders ready for salting and drying for a traditional pre-meal snack.

BOKKEMS

This favourite West Coast snack is a valuable source of protein for fishing communities. Visitors purchase them at local stores, and sample them at open-air restaurants where they hang in bunches to whet the appetite prior to a seafood feast. Bokkem slivers are great for garnishing soup. Another way to enjoy them is by soaking in water to reduce saltiness, then steaming in a little water in a covered pan.

**fresh harders, gutted and scaled
coarse sea salt**

Wash the fish thoroughly. Layer in a container, salting liberally as you go. Cover loosely with a cloth and leave overnight in a cool spot.

Rinse fish lightly. Hang in bunches to dry in a cool place where there's a good circulation of air; this should take about 10 days, depending on the weather. Bring bunches inside at night to protect them from the dew.

When dried and crisp enough for your liking, slice off snippets and offer as snacks.

MAIZE AND PEANUT SQUARES

These nutty nibbles are similar to mukhomo, which became popular in the old homeland of Venda in the Northern Province after groundnuts (peanuts) were introduced to tribal black diets. They are great with a chilled beer.

**2 green mealies or sweetcorn
melted butter
200 g roasted peanuts**

Strip leaves and silk from the mealies. Brush kernels with butter and roast over the coals (this imparts the best flavour), or boil, partially covered, for 10-15 minutes until tender in a pot of unsalted water.

Cut kernels from cobs and crush with the peanuts. A food processor works well, though pounding with a pestle and mortar is the traditional way of doing it. Pack firmly into a baking dish and chill. To serve, cut into 4-cm squares.
MAKES ABOUT 32

ROASTED PUMPKIN PIPS

Flavour-packed pumpkin pips are extremely popular in black communities, either served as snacks or to accompany maize meal porridge. They used to be sold at street markets but, sadly, this charming custom has been usurped by the availability of ubiquitous packeted potato crisps!

**500 g pumpkin pips
15 ml salt**

Wash pips well to remove the waxy coating and pat dry with a clean cloth.

Heat a dry frying pan, add pips and salt and cook over high heat for about 5 minutes until they crackle and become crisp and aromatic. Serve warm, or cool; store in an airtight container. Offer with drinks or scatter over a salad.
MAKES 500 GRAMS

VEGETABLE SAMOOSAS

These spicy appetizers were introduced to the country by Indian immigrants, and have been enthusiastically adopted by Cape Malays, who fill them with a wide variety of stuffings including lamb, beef, chicken and fish.

PASTRY
750 ml cake flour

5 ml salt

2 ml turmeric

15 ml vegetable oil

5 ml lemon juice or grape vinegar

250 ml cold water (approximate amount)

FILLING
vegetable oil

2 onions, finely chopped

2 potatoes, peeled and finely chopped

4 carrots, peeled and finely chopped

2 ml salt

15 ml ground cumin

2 ml chilli powder

5 ml dried ginger

5 ml crushed garlic

2 ml turmeric

250 ml peas

125 ml chopped fresh coriander leaves

Vegetable Samoosas and Chicken Satay (page 40), are offered as pre-dinner snacks in the elegant bar at Cybele Forest Lodge in Mpumalanga.

PASTRY Set the oven at 200°C. Sift together the flour, salt and turmeric. Mix in the oil and lemon juice or vinegar with enough of the cold water to make a stiff dough. Knead on a floured surface until nice and elastic.

Divide into twelve pieces and roll into balls. Roll out into 10-cm rounds (about the size of a saucer). Pile into four stacks of three, brushing the bottom two with oil and sprinkling with a little flour. (The top one should be ungreased and unfloured.) Roll out the stacks into very thin rectangles and trim sides neatly.

Arrange on ungreased baking trays and place in the oven for a few minutes until the dough puffs up slightly. While still hot, separate the sheets, cut into strips about 8-cm wide and 25-cm long, and cover with a damp cloth to prevent them from drying out.

FILLING Heat a little oil in a medium saucepan and fry the onion until translucent. Add the potato, carrot, salt, cumin, chilli, ginger, garlic and turmeric. Cover and cook for about 5 minutes until vegetables are tender. Add the peas and coriander and heat through. Allow to cool.

To make the samoosas, cut one end of the pastry strip on the diagonal and fold over twice to form a triangle. Fill the pocket with about 10 ml filling, then fold pastry across the top to seal the opening. Wet the remaining edge with water and pinch to seal. Set aside in a cool place for about 30 minutes, or cover and refrigerate for up to a day.

Deep fry samoosas in hot oil until crisp and golden. Drain well and serve warm or at room temperature.

MAKES ABOUT 36; SERVES 6-8

FISH SAMBAL

Recipes for gestampte snoek (pounded snoek) were brought to the Cape colony by Malay slaves in the seventeenth century. Interestingly, a similar 'fish cream' was popular amongst British travellers in the 1920s and 1930s, though their blander version was made without chilli and lemon, and was mixed with milk to the consistency of mashed potato. Snoek is preferred, though any fish may be substituted.

200 g cooked or smoked fish
50 g butter
1 onion, finely chopped
1 small green chilli, finely chopped
15 ml lemon juice
salt, milled black pepper

Skin, bone and flake the fish. Heat the butter in a frying pan and fry the onion and chilli until golden. Remove from heat, mix in the flaked fish and lemon juice, and season with salt and pepper. Scoop into a bowl, cover and refrigerate until firm. Serve liberally spread on wholewheat bread.
SERVES 4-6

CHICKEN SATAY

400 g filleted, skinless chicken breasts
vegetable oil
1 onion, finely chopped
5 ml crushed garlic
2 ml chilli powder
15 ml peanut butter
10 ml turmeric
5 ml brown sugar
45 ml soy sauce
15 ml lemon juice
200 ml water

Cut the chicken into strips and place in a non-metal dish. Heat a little oil in a medium saucepan and fry the onion and garlic until translucent. Stir in the remaining ingredients, cover and simmer for about 5 minutes. Allow to cool, then pour over the chicken. Cover and set aside in a cool spot for at least 2 hours to marinate, or refrigerate overnight.

Preheat oven griller. Thread meat evenly onto thin bamboo skewers and grill for 4-5 minutes on each side. Reheat the marinade and offer as a sauce.
SERVES 6-8

BLUE CHEESE MOUSSE WITH GREEN FIG PRESERVE

The Dutch are among the best cheese-makers in the world, a talent they brought with them when settling at the Cape. Green fig preserve is often served with cheese after a meal. Here is a variation on that theme.

15 ml gelatine
125 ml warm Chicken Stock (page 216)
250 g cream cheese
30 g blue cheese
125 ml Mayonnaise (page 218)
2 ml paprika
2 ml salt
125 ml cream
Green Fig Preserve (page 173)

Blue Cheese Mousse with Green Fig Preserve (page 173) on the menu of Old Halliwell Country Inn, in the tranquil KwaZulu-Natal midlands.

Sprinkle the gelatine on the surface of the warm chicken stock, allow to sponge, then stir until dissolved. Allow to cool. Purée together the cream cheese, blue cheese, mayonnaise, paprika and salt. Mix in the gelatine.

Whip the cream until stiff and fold gently into the mousse. Pour into six lightly-oiled ramekins (or one large mould), and chill for a few hours until set.

Just before serving, turn out the mousse/s and serve with green fig preserve. Garnish with sliced and seeded chilli.
SERVES 6

OLIVE SPREAD

This quick, easy recipe comes from Prince Albert, a tiny hamlet at the foot of the Swartberg range in the heart of the olive-growing region of the Karoo. Townsfolk are so proud of their famous crop that they hold an annual olive festival in its honour!

400 g black or calamata olives,
drained and pipped
4 hard-boiled eggs, shelled and quartered
30 ml olive oil

Purée all the ingredients in a food processor to form a paste. Serve with crisp biscuits or crusty bread.
SERVES 8

LOBSTER PATE

*This is a more modern version of the elementary baked terrine,
once made with pounded lobster meat mixed with
sheep's tail fat and spices. This rich and subtly
flavoured pâté is a dinner party favourite.*

3 lobster tails
500 ml water
small bunch fresh herbs
(parsley, thyme, oregano, bay leaf)
150 g butter
1 small onion, finely chopped
60 ml cream
30 ml brandy
grated nutmeg, cayenne pepper, salt

Shell and devein the lobster, and cut into smallish chunks.
Set aside while preparing the stock.

Crack shells into pieces and place in a small saucepan
with the water and herbs. Bring to the boil, then reduce
heat and simmer, uncovered, for 10-15 minutes until the
liquid has reduced to 30 ml. Strain and set aside.

Heat half the butter in a small frying pan and gently fry
the onion until golden. Add the lobster and cook gently for
2-3 minutes, until just cooked through.

Purée with the remaining butter and the reduced stock,
cream and brandy, and season with a little nutmeg, cayenne
pepper and salt. Spoon into small bowls (use a piping bag if
you wish) and chill for up to 3 days.

Garnish with lemon twists and serve at room temperature
with toast triangles.
SERVES 8-10

LOBSTER IN AVOCADO

We all remember avocado Ritz as a trendy starter in the 1960s. The idea, however, was formed a century earlier, when we served rock lobster on lettuce with a garnish of hard-boiled egg, sliced cucumber and lobster coral. Avocado makes a perfect receptacle; equally delicious substitutes include melon, pawpaw and papino. Monkfish may be added to plump out the more costly crustacean. If nasturtiums are flowering, add a few green seeds to the dressing to give it a lift.

3-4 lobster tails
3 ripe avocados
lemon juice
salt, milled black pepper
lemon wedges
SEAFOOD SAUCE
125 ml Mayonnaise (page 218)
60 ml plain yoghurt
30 ml tomato sauce
15 ml very finely chopped spring onion
1 ml ground ginger
1 ml ground coriander
2 ml finely chopped fresh thyme leaves

Cook the lobster tails in a small, covered saucepan of simmering water. This will take 3-4 minutes, depending on size. Shell, devein and cut meat into small cubes.

Cut the avocados in half; remove and discard pips. Slice slivers from rounded sides to enable them to stand level. Brush cut edges with lemon juice to prevent discolouration and season with salt and pepper. Place on serving plates.

Mix together the seafood sauce ingredients, season with salt and pepper, and mix in the lobster. Spoon into avocado hollows and place lemon wedges alongside.
SERVES 6

Green Asparagus with Spicy Mayonnaise pays homage to wild asparagus (nicknamed cat briar), which featured on early menus. A sauce similar to Spicy Mayonnaise was made by mashing hard-boiled egg yolks with mustard, salt, cream, vinegar and powdered chilli.

GREEN ASPARAGUS WITH SPICY MAYONNAISE

2 punnets green asparagus, rinsed and trimmed
4 hard-boiled eggs
SPICY MAYONNAISE
2 egg yolks
1 ml salt
2 ml chilli powder
2 ml dry English mustard
45 ml lemon juice
375 ml vegetable oil

Steam the asparagus over boiling water until tender, or simmer in lightly salted water in a covered saucepan – the spears should droop just a little when lifted. Drain well.
SPICY MAYONNAISE Place the egg yolks, salt, chilli powder and mustard in a food processor and whizz until thick. With the machine running, slowly add the lemon juice, then pour in the oil in a thin stream. Transfer to a bowl and chill. (It may be refrigerated for up to 3 days.)

Arrange portions of asparagus on serving plates and spoon over a little mayonnaise; offer the remainder separately. Garnish with quartered hard-boiled eggs.
SERVES 6-8

OSTRICH CARPACCIO
WITH MARINATED VEGETABLES

*Most locals wouldn't dream of eating raw meat, but
carpaccio has become a modern classic, fast gaining in
popularity. It may be prepared with ostrich, beef or venison.
Meat and vegetables may be prepared a couple of hours ahead.
Cover separately and keep chilled.*

250 g well-trimmed ostrich fillet

olive oil

1 small onion, sliced

1 red pepper, seeded and sliced

1 yellow pepper, seeded and sliced

3 cloves garlic, cut into slivers

30 ml drained capers

30 ml wine vinegar

finely grated rind and juice of ½ small lemon

salt, milled black pepper

Firm up the meat in the freezer (don't allow it to freeze).
Slice very finely – preferably with a meat or bread slicer –
and arrange in concentric overlapping circles on a plate. Seal
with plastic wrap and chill.

Heat a little olive oil in a frying pan and stir-fry the onion
until translucent. Add the red and yellow peppers and garlic, and stir-fry until limp. Remove from the heat, season
with salt and pepper, and add the capers.

Measure 60 ml olive oil into a bowl, whisk in the vinegar
and lemon juice and rind, and season with salt and pepper.
Pour over the vegetables, cover and chill.

TO SERVE   Arrange vegetables on the meat. Drizzle the
dressing over. Garnish, if you wish, with sliced rocket leaves.

SERVES 4

*Ostrich Carpaccio with Marinated Vegetables at
Bushman's Kloof Private Game Reserve in the
Cederberg range on the edge of the Great Karoo.*

Cut off and discard thick spinach stems and chop leaves roughly. Melt the butter in a large saucepan and fry the leek gently until softened. Add the apple and wet spinach, cover and steam for about 5 minutes, stirring occasionally. Pour in the stock, season with salt, pepper and nutmeg. Cover and simmer gently for about 20 minutes.

Purée the soup; pour into a clean pot. Add most of the cream, and lemon juice and reheat. Garnish with remaining cream.
SERVES 8

COOL AVOCADO SOUP WITH CORIANDER AND CHILLI JAM

Avocados originated in tropical South America and now grow in such diverse countries as Israel, California and Africa. In some countries like Ghana and Kenya every house has a tree, and villagers get bored with the fruit! This gently flavoured soup needs a careful hand with the stock – home-made is best; if using cubes or powder go easy on the amount, as the flavour can be dominating.

4-6 spring onions, trimmed
1 small bunch fresh coriander leaves,
well washed and dried
2 ripe avocados, skinned and pipped
500 ml weak Chicken Stock (page 216)
125 ml thick cream, plain yoghurt or buttermilk
salt and milled black pepper
Chilli Jam (page 169)

Pop the spring onion and coriander into a food processor and chop finely. Add the avocados, stock and cream, yoghurt or buttermilk, and blend until smooth. Season with salt and pepper. Cover and chill.

Top each bowl of soup with a dollop of chilli jam.
SERVES 4

SPINACH AND APPLE SOUP

Long before the arrival of European settlers, edible herbs and greens grew wild on the slopes of Table Mountain, and in the surrounding countryside. Soon the likes of sorrel, wateruintjie (water hawthorn), wild cabbage and spinach were being simmered into soup. Later seasonal cultivated vegetables were added. This dish reflects the fairly simple recipes of days gone by, and our enjoyment of mixing sweet and sour in one dish.

4 bunches spinach (about 1,2 kg),
well washed
50 g butter
4 leeks, finely sliced
2 Granny Smith apples, peeled, cored and chopped
1 litre hot Chicken Stock (page 216)
salt and milled black pepper
2 ml grated nutmeg
250 ml cream
lemon juice

MULLIGATAWNY SOUP

*This spicy soup has its origins in southern India, yet the recipe
was introduced to South Africa by early British food writers like
Mrs HM Slade and S van H Tulleken. They, in turn, had
learned it from the British Raj, who spent years in India as
army officers, civil servants and diplomats. Versions are many
and varied; this one is particularly delightful. Authenticate the
presentation by offering the soup with plain or spiced rice.*

1 chicken (about 1 kg), skinned

30 g tamarind seed

vegetable oil

4 onions, chopped

5 ml finely chopped garlic

1 green chilli, sliced and seeded

large sprigs fresh mint and thyme

60 ml chopped fresh parsley

2 ml ground mace

15 ml curry powder

1 large carrot, peeled and very finely diced

1 large turnip, peeled and very finely diced

4 apples peeled, cored and finely chopped

2,5 litres hot Meat Stock (page 216)

salt, milled black pepper

30 ml rice flour

200 ml semi-sweet white wine

Cut the chicken into smallish pieces, wash and pat dry.
Place the tamarind in a small bowl, add water to cover and
set aside to soak.

Heat a little oil in a large saucepan and fry the chicken,
onion and garlic until golden. Stir in the chilli, mint, thyme,
parsley, mace and curry powder. Add the carrot, turnip,
apple and stock. Season with salt and pepper, cover and
simmer for about 1 hour.

Drain soup into a clean saucepan through a colander.
Discard herbs, chilli and bones. Shred the meat and return
to the saucepan with the vegetables. Bring to the boil.

Sieve tamarind into a small bowl and discard the seed.
Mix in the rice flour. Stir into the soup until it thickens. Stir
in the wine and heat through.

SERVES 8-10

CURRIED FISH SOUP

*A cornerstone in villages where folk live off the sea, and who
never allow anything to go to waste. Flavours are faithful to
Cape Malay cooks, who count curried snoek-head soup amongst
their favourites. The best fish soup is made with several types of
fish. To make ahead, prepare soup prior to adding the fish.
Chill for up to a day, then reheat, add the fish and complete
the recipe. Ring the changes by garnishing with sliced hard-boiled
egg as it was done way back when.*

2-3 smallish fish (about 3 kg in total), filleted

(retain heads and bones)

butter, vegetable oil

2 onions, finely sliced

2 carrots, peeled and finely sliced

2 ribs celery, finely chopped

2 cloves garlic, very finely chopped

2 ml crushed green ginger

10 ml curry powder

1 red or green chilli, sliced and seeded

2 ml saffron threads, soaked in a little warm water,

or 2 ml turmeric

4 ripe tomatoes, blanched, skinned and chopped,

or 400 g can tomatoes, chopped (don't drain)

125 ml dry white wine

1,5 litres water

4 potatoes, peeled and finely diced

salt, milled black pepper

Rinse fish heads and bones. Skin fish and cut into chunks.

Heat a little butter and oil in a large saucepan and fry the
onion, carrot, celery, garlic and ginger until golden. Stir in
the curry powder, chilli and saffron or turmeric. Add the
tomato, wine, water and fish heads and bones. Cover and
simmer for about 20 minutes.

Remove and discard bones and heads. Add the potato and
season with salt and pepper. Cover and simmer for about
10 minutes until soft. Add the fish, cover and simmer for
about 5 minutes until cooked. Check and adjust the flavour
if necessary. Serve with brown bread and a garnish of coriander leaves, if you wish.

SERVES 8-10

PUMPKIN SOUP

1 kg skinned pumpkin, pipped and cut into cubes
2 onions, chopped
2 thin slices green ginger
1 litre Chicken Stock (page 216)
salt, milled black pepper
1 ml grated nutmeg
30 ml cake flour
30 ml soft butter
250 ml cream

Combine the pumpkin, onion, ginger and stock in a large saucepan. Season with salt, pepper and nutmeg. Cover and simmer for about 30 minutes until vegetables are soft.

Strain (reserve liquid), and purée vegetables with a little of the liquid. Mix flour and butter into the purée.

Pour back into the pot with the remaining liquid and stir over medium heat for 1-2 minutes until the soup thickens. Add the cream, check the flavour and adjust if necessary.

Ladle soup into warm bowls and garnish, if you wish, with swirls of cream and a sprinkling of chopped fresh herbs.

SERVES 6-8

PEA SOUP WITH SMOKED PORK

Ertjiesop (pea soup) originated in Holland,
and the recipe was fine-tuned by Cape Malays.
However, as pork is haraam (forbidden) to all Muslims,
they would use beef or lamb and not smoked
pork knuckles, which are favoured by Germans and other
mid-European folk.

250 g dried split peas
2 smoked pork knuckles or soup meat
2 litres hot Chicken Stock (page 216)
1 onion, finely chopped
2 ribs celery, finely sliced
1 large carrot, peeled and finely chopped

3 whole cloves
2 whole allspice
5 ml dry English mustard
salt, milled black pepper

Place the split peas and pork knuckles or soup meat in a large saucepan. Add the stock, cover, and simmer for about 1½ hours. Skim off any scum that surfaces.

Add the onion, celery, carrot, cloves, allspice and mustard, and season with salt and pepper. Cover and simmer for about 30 minutes until vegetables are soft. Check the consistency; add a little water if the soup is too thick. Check and adjust the flavour if necessary. Remove the fat and break up the meat before serving, so that everyone gets a chunk.
SERVES 8

CHICKEN SOUP

This is a free adaptation of the many variations of this popular soup. Mace is replaced by cardamom and saffron or turmeric, perfect foils for the undertones of coconut. Optional garnishes include fresh coriander leaves or sprigs of watercress, which grew wild in water furrows at the Cape, and were used with various wild lettuces in our earliest salads. A handful of crushed, roasted peanuts stirred in at the end is another African-style idea.

1 chicken
butter, salt, milled black pepper
1 large onion, chopped
2 carrots, sliced
1 rib celery, sliced
1 bunch fresh herbs
(parsley, bay leaf, fennel)
6 cardamom pods, lightly crushed
2 ml saffron threads, soaked in a
little warm water, or 2 ml turmeric
2 litres hot Chicken Stock (page 216)
250 ml cooked rice
250 ml coconut cream
2 egg yolks
250 ml cream

Joint the chicken, wash well and pat dry. Heat a little butter in a large saucepan and lightly brown chicken all over. Season with salt and pepper and stir in the onion, carrot, celery, herbs, cardamom and saffron or turmeric. Pour in the stock, cover and simmer gently for about 45 minutes until chicken is cooked.

Remove chicken from the pot and allow to cool. Remove and discard skin and bones, shred meat finely, cover and set aside. Strain stock into a clean pot, add the rice, cover and simmer for about 20 minutes until very soft.

Add the coconut cream and chicken meat and bring to the boil. Mix together the egg yolks and cream, stir in and remove from the heat before the soup comes to the boil again. Serve piping hot.
SERVES 10

BEAN SOUP

Any type of dried beans may be used in hearty boontjiesop, an age-old recipe that is believed to have its roots in northern Germany and which was introduced to the Cape via Holland. It is still a favourite on winter menus of many homes and country hotels. Early recipes called for white sauce to be stirred in, while the Cape Malay version is served with dumplings and includes a small green chilli and a sliver of green ginger in the line-up of interesting spicings.

250 ml dried beans, well rinsed
2 litres weak Meat Stock (page 216)
500 g beef shin (on the bone)
100 g rindless streaky bacon, chopped
1 onion, finely chopped
1 turnip, peeled and finely chopped
1 carrot, peeled and finely chopped
2 ripe tomatoes, blanched, skinned and chopped
salt and milled black pepper
lemon juice

Place the beans in a large saucepan, cover generously with cold water, and set aside for about 12 hours to soak and plump. If you are pressed for time, bring to the boil, then set aside for 1-2 hours.

Drain beans, return to the saucepan and add the stock, beef shin and bacon. Cover and simmer gently for 1 hour. Add the onion, turnip and carrot and cook for 1-1½ hours more until beans are mushy.

Drain soup over a bowl and discard bones and fat. Push beans, vegetables and soup through a sieve into a clean saucepan, or process in a food processor; don't make it too fine – the texture should be rough. Add the liquid and the chopped tomato. Check the flavour and season with salt and pepper. Cover and simmer for about 10 minutes more. Add a squeeze of lemon juice just before serving.
SERVES 8

LOBSTER BISQUE

Rock lobsters, abundant in southern and eastern coastal
waters, have been turned into tasty meals since way back.
This excellent soup was recorded by C Louis Leipoldt,
a master of the early Cape table, who credits a
'very expert coloured woman' as his mentor.
She, of course, honed her skills by observing Cape Malay
cooks in action. The entire lobster is used, including the shell,
which is slowly simmered to make an exquisite stock.
Early cooks plumped it up with cooked rice, chopped
tomato and finely diced potato, and spiced
it with curry powder.

1 large lobster
50 g soft butter
1 ml mace
4 rashers rindless bacon,
finely chopped
2 carrots, peeled and very finely chopped
2 onions, very finely chopped
2 ml crushed garlic
2-3 thin slices green ginger
2 lemon leaves, lightly crushed
sprig fresh thyme
small piece lemon rind
salt, milled black pepper
500 ml dry white wine
500 ml water
2 egg yolks
60 ml medium-dry sherry
125 ml cream

Split the lobster in half down its length and lift out and discard the alimentary canal. Remove flesh, including coral and soft white and green parts under the body shell, as well as flesh from the larger claws.

Slice or dice tail meat, place in a bowl and chill. Place remaining meat with coral and green meat in a food processor with half the butter and the mace. Purée, cover and chill in the fridge.

Chop the shells into small pieces and set aside. Melt the remaining butter in a large saucepan and stir in the bacon,

carrot, onion, garlic, ginger, lemon leaves, thyme and lemon rind. Cover and simmer gently for about 20 minutes until everything is nice and soft.

Season with salt and pepper, pour in the wine and water and add the pieces of lobster shell. Cover and simmer gently for about 1 hour. Strain into a clean saucepan, pressing out all the liquid. Bring to the boil, stir in the lobster purée, then add the tail meat. Cook for 1-2 minutes more.

Mix together the egg yolks and sherry and stir in with the cream. Remove from the heat immediately (don't let the soup boil), check the flavour and adjust if necessary.
SERVES 6

SPICED TOMATO SOUP

This palate-tickling version of tomato soup is the way our
Indian community prefers it, although you are welcome to omit
the chilli if you don't like things hot. The soup may be made
a day or two ahead; cover and chill.

50 g butter
1 onion, finely chopped
1 kg ripe tomatoes, blanched, skinned
and chopped
30 ml cake flour
1 litre hot Chicken Stock (page 216)
1 small green chilli, seeded and finely chopped
5 ml paprika
5 ml sugar
2 cinnamon sticks
2 whole cloves
1 bay leaf, lightly crushed
salt, milled black pepper

Melt the butter in a large saucepan and fry the onion gently until translucent. Add the tomato, flour, stock, chilli, paprika, sugar, cinnamon, cloves and bay leaf, and season with salt and pepper. Cover and simmer for about 30 minutes.

Discard cinnamon and bay leaf, and purée the soup, or leave chunky if preferred. Serve hot or chilled, plain or garnished with a swirl of thick cream.
SERVES 6-8

BLACK MUSSEL SOUP

36 black mussels, well scrubbed
500 ml water
50 g butter
1 onion, chopped
2 ml crushed garlic
45 ml cake flour
500 ml hot Fish Stock (page 216)
125 ml dry white wine
30 ml chopped fresh parsley
1 bay leaf or lemon leaf, lightly crushed
1 ml grated nutmeg
milled black pepper
125 ml cream

Place the mussels and water in a saucepan, cover and boil until they open. Remove from the pot and set aside. Retain 250 ml of the mussel liquor. Detach mussels from shells, pull out and discard beards and chop meat finely. Alternatively leave them whole, with or without their shells.

Heat the butter in a clean saucepan and fry the onion and garlic until translucent. Remove from the heat and blend in the flour, then the mussel liquor, fish stock and wine. Stir over medium heat until the soup thickens. Add the parsley and bay or lemon leaf, and season with nutmeg and pepper. Add salt only if necessary; mussels are naturally salty. Cover and simmer very gently for 10 minutes.

Just before serving, add the cream and mussels and heat through without allowing the soup to boil.
SERVES 6-8

CHAPTER FIVE
WEST COAST
& NAMAQUALAND

TORTOISES AND TUMBLEWEEDS; SHIPWRECKS AND SEAFOOD

THE REMOTE, SUN-SPLASHED, wind-lashed western area of the Cape Province is a place of contrasts, contradictions and timeless beauty. It was here that the seeds of our multi-cultural history were sown, and here that Westcoasters learnt to triumph over a harsh climate and an uncompromising environment, for the benefit of future generations.

On these shores Portuguese seafarers first encountered Africa's earliest inhabitants, described by one scribe as 'swarthy men who eat only sea wolves and whales, and the flesh of gazelles, and the roots of plants and honey.' The sailors were tracking ancient legends about a mystical world deep in the southern Atlantic, voyages of discovery spurred on by the desire to trade, which preceded the establishment of a sea route to the Indies.

The vastness, flatness and silence of this seemingly barren place strike you first; from one horizon to the other little disturbs the line of vision. Stay awhile. Stroll along a beach and feel the sand between your toes. Wander through the wilds. You will discover a world with an unparalleled culinary ethic, for folk here cling fast to their heritage, and uphold a regional integrity unlike anywhere else.

As the urban jungle fades in the distance, your mood shifts from city stress to spacial serenity, for this is the ultimate bolt-hole for those bored by the hype of city living. Life trundles along at a snail's pace. There are no pretensions of grandeur except for a breathtaking, natural marvel each spring: briefly, after winter rains have soaked the veld and worked their magic, wild flowers bloom in an almost

 A successful day's catch: baskets filled with rock lobsters aboard a fishing boat lying at anchor in Lambert's Bay.

indecent array of glory, too soon to fade into the oblivion of the vast, monochromatic landscape. The fynbos is precious in that, as part of the Cape floral kingdom, it is the largest remaining tract of natural vegetation of its type in the world.

Economical, social and geographic factors create a unique arena for culinary individuality. The land is locked between the icy Atlantic Ocean and the rugged mountains of the Bokkeveld and Cederberg, stretching north to the desert's doorstep and the Great Karoo. Areas are known by time-honoured names like Swartland, Strandveld, Hantam, Knersvlakte, Voor-Boesmanland, Hardeveld, Richtersveld and Sandveld, a narrow coastal strip forming a natural buffer between sea and inland regions.

For thousands of years this was home to the San (Bushmen), Khoikhoi (Hottentots), Strandlopers, and Nama people, after whom Namaqualand was named. Historians named these genetically similar people Khoisan. Artful hunter-gatherers, they neither planted nor reaped crops, but bagged wild game and scratched a meagre existence from seashore and scrub, brewed intoxicating liquor from roots, roasted fruits and infused them for beverages, taught their children which berries, seeds and corms to pluck for snacks, which to suck for a special treat, and which to bring home to be made into syrup.

Indigenous food legends live on, passed down from one generation to the next. Wild figs are eaten fresh and made into jam; Cape sorrel is simmered into soup and added to stews; pelargonium petals are used as a herb; various spinach-type plants, like hotnotskool (Hottentots' cabbage, 'better than asparagus') and kinkelbossie (twisted bush) are added to bredies.

Seafood, nourished by the icy Benguela current that sweeps the coast, has always sustained local folk. Testimonies to this are the middens of fish bones, shells and the like, left behind by the Strandlopers. Their catch was either eaten immediately (perhaps grilled over open coals) or preserved by drying and salting.

Weathered folk still pit their skills against Nature to catch anchovies, snoek, galjoen, hottentot, silverfish, white stumpnose, elf, harders, kabeljou, geelbek, rock lobsters (crayfish), and perlemoen (abalone). Some seasons are better than others, creating an uncertainty well understood by fisherfolk the world over.

TOP *Busy fishermen sort boxes of Cape rock lobster.*
BOTTOM *A cluster of dinghies at the jetty at Elands Bay.*

ABOVE *Gathering waterblommetjies at Voëlvlei Farm at Piketberg. This unique vegetable has bloomed in vleis, dams and streams for centuries, and farmers now cultivate it for cash crops. Up to two tons a week are dispatched from this farm during the winter season.*
LEFT *Strandkombuis open-air seafood restaurant overlooking Sixteen Mile Beach at Yzerfontein.*

Harbours dotting the coastline provide safe havens for boats, and factories to process their catch – filleting, freezing, smoking, drying, canning, grinding into fish meal and rendering it into oil. Lambert's Bay, focus of the rock lobster (crayfish) industry, has one of the prettiest harbours of all, which forms a bridge to Bird Island, breeding place of the Cape gannet and cormorant, just two of the myriad types of feathered creatures that call the West Coast home.

Further south is Saldanha Bay, where marvellous molluscs like mussels and oysters are farmed. Oysters originated way, way back, creating an interesting puzzle to ponder: fossilized shells of an extinct warm-water oyster have been found in northern Namaqualand and the Langebaan lagoon, their demise caused by some major climactic change long before the coastline's history was written. Those in the lagoon are estimated at 30 tons, making it the largest oyster graveyard in the world. Mussel farming, a more recent innovation as black mussels are still easily gathered from rocks at low tide, follows the simple Spanish 'raft and rope' technology.

Open-air restaurants, hosted by locals whose love of (and respect for) seafood is as legendary as their enthusiasm for entertaining, are a feature of coastal towns. Guests gather casually to feast on copious quantities of seafood and appease sea-breeze-sharpened appetites. Perlemoen bisque is ladled from huge pots. Rows of golden snoek are generously sploshed with garlicky butter as they sizzle over open coals. Hot-smoked linefish emerges from smokers. Mammoth loaves of bread are baked in traditional bakoonde (ovens); farm butter and home-made konfyt (jam) are ready for spreading. Trays are piled with black mussels and rock lobster (crayfish) fresh from the ocean. Bredies are cosseted in potjies – the same fat-bellied, three-legged pots that accompanied people in the past, on their treks through the country. Ingredients patiently simmer away to that inevitable stage where meat and sauce merge into a delicious union, and vegetables are unashamedly mushy.

Protein-rich bokkems (from the Dutch *bokking*, meaning herring) are a popular local snack. Small fish like harders are salted, tied in bunches and dried like biltong. Fishermen rely on bokkems to predict a change in the weather; when they drip, rain will fall within a day! The practical explanation has more to do with reason than folklore – the high salt content of the fish combines with the increased humidity of the air to produce the effect.

If dried fish isn't your idea of heaven, you may prefer other local delights like peertjies (spiced lamb's testicles), pofadders (lamb's intestines filled with offal and cooked over the coals), or skilpadjies – caul fat similarly stuffed and cooked.

TOP *Young boys at Elands Bay proudly show their catch.*
BOTTOM *Bird-shooting in the Swartland wheatfields.*

Happily, tortoises – from which skilpadjies get their name – are no longer turned into soup. Now protected, they are free to roam in peace, and road signs request motorists to stop if they see one and carry it to the safety of the fynbos!

Twigs and leaves of the rooibos (red bush), which occurs along the Olifants River and high in the Cederberg, are dried and made into a tannin-free tea; it is farmed nowhere else in the world. Mountain folk were probably drinking it centuries ago; today it is the preferred beverage, not only of locals (who claim to be the best rooibos-brewers in the land, and who always have a pot of rooibos simmering on the stove), but many South Africans and health-conscious folk all over the world.

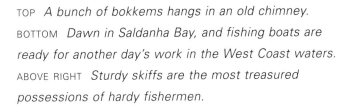

TOP *A bunch of bokkems hangs in an old chimney.*
BOTTOM *Dawn in Saldanha Bay, and fishing boats are ready for another day's work in the West Coast waters.*
ABOVE RIGHT *Sturdy skiffs are the most treasured possessions of hardy fishermen.*

Waterblommetjies (little water flowers) bloom in vleis, dams and streams. This unique vegetable has been informally harvested for centuries; now farmers grow plants in specially prepared ponds. There are other indigenous foods to enjoy, like uintjies (peel, boil and enjoy their chestnut-peanut flavour) and heerbone (the Lord's beans), which pad out homely bredies and curries. Sandveld sugar pumpkins, with skin the colour of rich Kalahari soil and flesh of yellow, make 'the best fritters in the world', traditionally flavoured with lemon rind and cinnamon, and studded with raisins.

Throughout most of the region soil is too poor to sustain agriculture to any great extent, except in the lush Olifants River Valley, where groves of citrus grow, and the Swartland – named after the dark soil and scrublike vegetation – which is the hub of a rich wheat industry and heart of the wine route that sprawls from Malmesbury in the south to Mamre,

Riebeek Kasteel, Riebeek West, Porterville, Piketberg and Citrusdal. The wines of the Olifants River Wine Route – like folk around here – are unpretentious and friendly; made for casual quaffing rather than competitions and cellar-ageing.

The Khoisan are long gone; elephants and antelope no longer run wild and free and, thanks to plundering whalers, these gentle giants of the deep are few and far between. Yet, even compared with other quiet corners of the country, this western one feels least the impact of man. Highways and byways are relatively free of hordes of tourists, unspoilt beaches are uncrowded and unlittered, and life slips by much the way it has done for many, many years.

West Coast doors are open to friends who find time to pop in for a cup of tea or a *dop* or two of something stronger. Guest houses offer country-style hospitality in keeping with the laid-back mood, and restaurants specialize in the freshest seafood to be found anywhere in the country, plainly cooked and designed to fill tummies rather than tease tastebuds and please the eye in the mode of city cuisine.

When your pace has slowed to the West Coast beat and you take your leave of this placid land, it will be with the hope that not much will change before you return for another glimpse of the simple life, and another taste of homely dishes that are faithful to recipes of days gone by.

CHAPTER SIX
SALADS, GRAINS & VEGETABLES

IN THE TRADITIONAL AFRICAN diet, plant protein assumes an importance that other cuisines place on either seafood or meat. Unrefined cereals and grains, nutritious legumes, simply cooked vegetables and raw fruit play a starring role; meat, sugar, salt and added fat are conspicuous by their absence. In short, a healthy food regime nutritionists encourage the world at large to follow.

The cultivation of vegetables by tribal farmers was noted in sailors' writings of 1554, which tell of crops like maize, millet, melons, beans, gourds, sugar cane and grain sorghum – used as a grain as well as in the brewing of beer.

LEFT *Salad Leaves with an Old-Fashioned Dressing (page 63), on the front stoep of the Artists' Cafe at the old railway station at Hendriksdal in Mpumalanga.* ABOVE *Slaphakskeentjies (page 64), a traditional onion dish, which may be served hot or cool.*

All South Africans – including the San (Bushmen), rural blacks, wandering pastoralists and trek-farmers – relied on plant food from the veld in past times. Mothers taught their daughters which bulbs, shoots, roots, seeds, flowers and leaves to use, and, more importantly, which are poisonous.

Best known veld food is morogo or imfino, which is, in fact, the leaves of more than a hundred different varieties of plants. The leaves, pods and tendrils vary in flavour, and are carefully plucked so as not to damage the plant.

Protein-rich legumes have long grown in rural gardens and on farms, specifically cowpeas (which, despite its name, is a bean), jugobeans and mungbeans. Groundnuts, or peanuts (from northern areas of the continent), and pumpkin (from America), are more recent additions to African cookery.

Young fruit and leaves of hard-skinned gourds are delicious (the flavour is reminiscent of mushrooms), while pods are used as calabashes, eating vessels and household containers. Skilled hands dry or bake them to strengthen the skin, then cut an opening, scoop out the insides, and clean them by swirling with hard pebbles, sand or seeds.

The art of vegetable cooking took a turn when the Dutch planted their famous vegetable gardens at the Cape, bringing with them an abundance of vegetable seeds, and preparing the resultant crops in the seventeenth-century European manner. Favourite methods included droogkook (shallow frying in butter or fat), boiling and mashing, and creaming (simmering in cream). Glazing in bouillon with lavish quantities of butter and sugar was an early Cape-Dutch method of cooking, and one that is still enjoyed today.

From the earliest days, salads were popular, just as they are today. Wild leaves such as mustard, watercress, various wild lettuces, and soft young shoots of the palmiet bulrush formed a simple, fresh mélange. Roots, stems and leaves of sorrel added a sourish tang, and were also used as a substitute for lemons and vinegar.

Mpumalanga Salad Platter on a carpet of jacaranda flowers, at Cybele Forest Lodge, Mpumalanga.

SALAD LEAVES WITH AN OLD-FASHIONED DRESSING

Watercress, an early salad ingredient, proliferated along waterways in the Cape Peninsula and Boland. With the variety of salad leaves and herbs now at our disposal, one can make this recipe even more interesting.

mixed salad leaves and fresh herbs
OLD-FASHIONED DRESSING
1 hard-boiled egg yolk, mashed
100 ml red wine vinegar
60 ml vegetable oil
1 ml dry English mustard
salt, sugar

Wash and dry the salad leaves and herbs and toss in a salad bowl. Mash the egg yolk and whisk in the vinegar, oil and mustard. Season with salt and sugar. Pour over the salad and toss gently just before serving.
SERVES 6

MPUMALANGA SALAD PLATTER

Salads as starters or main dishes have become very much part of summer menus, and may be varied to suit whatever ingredients are at hand. This salad pays homage to the glorious ingredients that are special to the Mpumalanga Lowveld.

mixed salad leaves, herbs and edible flowers
200 g thinly sliced smoked trout
1-2 ripe avocados
lemon juice
1 orange, peeled and segments cut out
50 g macadamia nuts
50 g pecan nuts
trout caviare
HERB VINAIGRETTE
125 ml vegetable oil (or half vegetable, half olive oil)
30 ml lemon juice
30 ml wine vinegar
2 ml sugar
1 ml crushed garlic (optional)
salt, milled black pepper
1 ml dry English mustard
30 ml chopped fresh herbs

Make individual salads or one large platter. Use leaves as a base and top with curls of smoked trout. Peel, stone and slice the avocados and brush with lemon juice to prevent discolouring. Arrange on the salad with orange segments, nuts, sprigs of herbs, and edible flowers.
HERB VINAIGRETTE Whisk together the ingredients. Store in the fridge until required. Whisk again shortly before dressing the salad. Garnish with scoops of trout caviare. Serve with crusty bread.
SERVES 4

BEETROOT AND ONION SALAD

A side dish particularly well-loved by the Afrikaner community. Sliced chilli adds a Cape-Malay and Indian slant to the recipe. The flavour improves with keeping for a couple of days after preparation.

6-8 medium beetroot, washed
125 ml red wine vinegar
60 ml water
30 ml brown sugar
1 bay leaf
2 ml black peppercorns
5 ml salt
1 onion, finely sliced

Cut off the beetroot leaves, leaving a little of the stem intact to prevent 'bleeding' into the cooking water. Cover with cold water, bring to the boil and cook, partially covered, for about 45 minutes until tender. Drain, remove skins and slice beetroot into a bowl.

Combine the vinegar, water, brown sugar, bay leaf, peppercorns, salt and onion in a medium saucepan. Cover and bring to the boil. Pour over the beetroot and allow to cool.
SERVES 6

Slaphakskeentjies, Salad Leaves with an Old-Fashioned Dressing (page 63), Beetroot and Onion Salad (page 63).

SLAPHAKSKEENTJIES

If serving warm, make the sauce just before serving.

1 kg pickling onions, peeled
3 eggs
30 ml sugar
5 ml dry English mustard
2 ml salt
125 ml grape vinegar
30 ml water
200 ml milk or cream

Cook the onions in salted, boiling water until just tender but not overcooked. Drain and keep warm or allow to cool.

Whisk the eggs, sugar, mustard and salt in a medium saucepan with a hand whisk until frothy. Add the vinegar, water and milk or cream, and cook very gently over low heat, stirring constantly, until the sauce thickens. Pour over the onions and serve at once, or allow to cool.

SERVES 6-8

FREE STATE QUINCE SALAD

2 quinces (about 500 g)
2 ribs celery, finely sliced (use leaves as well)
15 ml cornflour
15 ml sugar
30 ml cider or wine vinegar

Gently rub the down off the quinces under running water. Peel, core and slice fairly finely. Place in a bowl of salted water (1 litre water with 15 ml salt) and set aside for about 30 minutes. Drain in a colander and tip into a saucepan. Add the celery and fresh water to cover the fruit. Cover and simmer for about 15 minutes until tender.

Drain fruit. Place in a bowl. Measure 300 ml cooking water and mix in the cornflour, sugar and vinegar. Boil, uncovered, until clear. Pour over the quinces. Serve cool.
SERVES 6

SOUSBOONTJIES

Sousboontjies, or 'sauced beans', are freely available at supermarkets but they are easy and satisfying to make at home.

500 g dried white kidney beans
50 g butter
60 ml sugar
125 ml grape vinegar
5 ml salt
2 ml white pepper

Wash the beans and soak overnight in plenty of cold water. Drain, add fresh water – just enough to immerse the beans – cover and simmer very gently for about 60 minutes until tender. (Cooking time depends on the age of the beans.)

Stir in the remaining ingredients and simmer, uncovered, until the sauce thickens slightly and the beans are soft yet still whole. This should take approximately 30 minutes. Stir occasionally. The sauce thickens as it cools.

Spoon hot sousboontjies into hot sterilised jars, seal and store in a dark, cool cupboard. Once opened, keep refrigerated.
MAKES ABOUT 2,5 LITRES

CARROT SALAD

500 g carrots, cut into slim batons

1 small red or green chilli, finely sliced and seeded

1 onion, finely sliced

125 ml water

125 ml red wine vinegar

60 ml vegetable oil

100 ml sugar

5 ml Worcestershire sauce

2 ml prepared English mustard

Cook the carrots in a little salted water until crisp but tender. Refresh under cold running water and tip into a bowl.

Combine the remaining ingredients in a saucepan and bring to the boil, stirring until the sugar dissolves. Pour hot sauce over carrots and set aside for 1-2 hours to marinate. Serve cool.

SERVES 4-6

TOMATO, EGG AND ONION SALAD

2-3 large, ripe tomatoes, sliced

3 hard-boiled eggs, sliced

1 onion, finely sliced, blanched and drained

10 ml cumin seeds, lightly roasted

in a dry pan

2 ml salt

5 ml sugar

60 ml herb or wine vinegar

15 ml lemon juice

30 ml vegetable oil

Arrange the tomato and hard-boiled eggs on a plate with the onion. Grind cumin seeds, salt and sugar with a pestle and mortar. Tip into a bowl and whisk in the vinegar, lemon juice and oil. Pour over the salad.

SERVES 6

SALADS, GRAINS & VEGETABLES

AVOCADO, SPINACH AND PAWPAW WITH ORANGE AND CUMIN DRESSING

A modern merging of traditional (spinach or morogo) and regional (pawpaw and avocados) ingredients discovered at Makalali Private Game Reserve on the banks of the Makhutswi river, close to the Drakensberg in the north-eastern Mpumalanga Lowveld.

1 bunch young spinach leaves, stems removed, washed and well dried, or morogo
2 ripe avocados, peeled, stoned and sliced
30 ml lemon juice
1 medium, ripe pawpaw, peeled, seeded and diced
1 red onion, thinly sliced
ORANGE AND CUMIN DRESSING
125 ml olive oil
30 ml red wine vinegar
90 ml orange juice (about 1½ oranges)
30 ml lime or lemon juice
15 ml cumin seeds, lightly roasted in a dry pan
salt, milled black pepper

Arrange the spinach or morogo in a large bowl. Brush the avocado with lemon juice and arrange on top with the pawpaw and onion. Whisk together the dressing ingredients. Pour over the salad just before serving.
SERVES 6

MAIZE MEAL AND SPINACH

This is a free adaptation of a tribal recipe, using spinach in place of wild morogo. If you wish, add chopped, salted peanuts as well, just before serving.

200 ml maize rice
1 bunch spinach, well washed
750 ml boiling water
250 ml maize meal
5 ml salt
2 ml turmeric

Place the maize rice in a bowl, add cold water to cover generously and set aside to soak for 4-6 hours. Drain and rinse.

Finely shred the spinach leaves and stems. Measure the boiling water into a medium saucepan and add the spinach, drained maize rice, maize meal, salt and turmeric. Stir until the water comes to the boil, then cover and cook over very gentle heat for about 20 minutes. Serve hot.

MAIZE MEAL AND SPINACH PATTIES Form the mixture into patties and fry in butter and oil. Serve warm.
SERVES 8-10

STAMPKORING WITH ONION, TOMATO AND NUTS

Pearled whole wheat is a nutty alternative to rice and, while normally served simply boiled, is easy to upgrade into something really special, similar to the different ways of preparing Italian risotto.

200 g (250 ml) stampkoring (pearled whole wheat)
750 ml Chicken Stock (page 216), or water
2 ml salt
2 onions, chopped
30 g (30 ml) butter
1 small green pepper, seeded and chopped
3-4 ripe tomatoes, blanched, skinned and chopped
2 ml turmeric
100 g cashew nuts or roasted peanuts

Rinse the stampkoring with cold water and place in a saucepan with the stock or water, and salt. Cover and simmer gently for about 40 minutes until tender. Drain.

Lightly brown the onion in the butter in a clean saucepan. Add the green pepper, tomato and turmeric and cook for a few minutes more. Stir in the drained stampkoring and heat through. Add the nuts just before serving.
SERVES 6

SAFFRON SAMP WITH CORN

*It is fascinating to explore recipes for staples like samp
and corn as prepared by different ethnic groups. Here the black
predilection for cooking samp with beans is altered to the white
preference for corn; a touch of saffron indicates a Cape-Malay
and Indian influence. Soaking samp shortens the cooking time.
Alternatively, simply cook it for a little longer.*

250 ml samp, well rinsed
5 ml saffron threads
750 ml boiling water
5 ml salt
340 g can whole kernel corn, drained
30 g (30 ml) butter

Tip samp into a saucepan. Add cold water to cover generously, cover and set aside to soak for about 8 hours. Drain well.

Soak the saffron in a little of the boiling water. Bring
remaining water to the boil in a medium saucepan, add
samp and saffron (with soaking water), cover and cook gently for about 1½ hours until tender. Replenish the water
from time to time if necessary. Add the salt towards the end
of the cooking time. Drain excess water, add drained corn
and butter and heat through. Tip into a warm serving bowl.
SERVES 6-8

Tip the beans and samp into a medium saucepan. Add cold water to cover. Cover and set aside to soak for about 8 hours. Drain well. (If you don't pre-soak, increase the cooking time.)

Bring 1,5 litres of water to the boil in the saucepan. Add samp and beans, cover and cook gently for about 1½ hours, replenishing the water when necessary. Add the salt towards the end of the cooking time.

Meanwhile set the oven at 220°C. Cut the tomatoes in half and place on a foil-lined baking tray. Roast uncovered for about 30 minutes until slightly dry and crisp. Lightly brown the onion in the butter in a frying pan.

Drain samp and beans, tip into a warm bowl and gently mix in the onion and tomatoes. Serve hot.
SERVES 8

BATSWANA CORN BAKE

From a small collection of recipes from the people of the region previously known as Bophuthatswana – now incorporated in the North West Province – comes this unique, delicious 'pudding'.

4 green mealies or sweetcorn
2 eggs, lightly beaten
2 ml salt
1 ml grated nutmeg
250 ml cream
30 g (30 ml) butter
1 small onion, finely chopped

Set the oven at 180°C. Butter a 1 litre oven-to-table casserole. Cut the kernels from the corn, chop finely, and mix in the eggs, salt, nutmeg and cream. Heat the butter in a small saucepan. Add the onion and fry until translucent. Add to the corn mixture. Pour into the buttered casserole, cover with oiled foil, and bake for about 1 hour until firm. Uncover for the last 15 minutes to brown the topping. Serve hot.
SERVES 6-8

SAMP AND BEANS

Gnush or umngqusho, a daily staple in black communities, is offered at celebratory menus from weddings to harvest festivals. Xhosa people are particularly fond of it, preferring it even to porridge. Two indigenous varieties of beans – jugo bean and cowpeas – were used in the past; any dried beans may be substituted. The only traditional addition is salt. Oven-crisped tomatoes and fried onion add flavour. If you wish, add a can of whole kernel corn, or some roasted peanuts.

250 ml dried kidney beans, rinsed
250 ml samp, rinsed
1,5 litres boiling water
7 ml salt
500 g small tomatoes
2 onions, thickly sliced in wedges
30 g (30 ml) butter

CORN DUMPLINGS
WITH CHILLI TOMATO

*An adaptation of dumplings the way the early black
tribes prepared them – fresh corn kernels, which women would
pound on a grinding stone, wrap in maize or pumpkin leaves
and steam in a pot. Sticks were ingeniously criss-crossed on the
base to lift them above the simmering water. Sometimes mashed
pumpkin was added. Chilli tomato updates the recipe.*

8 large spinach leaves, well washed
4 green mealies or sweetcorn
1 bunch fresh coriander leaves,
well washed and dried
125 ml cake flour
10 ml baking powder
5 ml salt
1 egg, lightly beaten
CHILLI TOMATO
2-3 large, ripe tomatoes, finely chopped
1 small onion, finely chopped
2 ml crushed garlic (optional)
1-2 red chillies, very finely chopped
30 ml olive oil
15 ml wine vinegar
5 ml sugar
2 ml salt

Blanch the spinach leaves in boiling water. Drain and place
on a work surface. Cut kernels from the corn and crush
finely (in a food processor or with a mortar and pestle). Mix
half the coriander into the corn. Reserve the remainder.

Sift the flour, baking powder and salt into the corn mixture, add the egg and mix in. Form into eight flattish patties, place on the spinach leaves and wrap neatly. Steam
over simmering water for 20 minutes. Serve hot or cool.
CHILLI TOMATO Mix together all the ingredients, cover
and set aside for at least 2 hours for the flavours to mingle.
Chill. Stir in the reserved coriander just before serving.

STYWEPAP WITH CHILLI TOMATO Serve Stywepap
(page 21) with Chilli Tomato, to accompany braaied meat.
SERVES 8

CORN FRITTERS

*Tradition dictates that, for these vetkoek, kernels are sliced from
corn cobs; a can of whole kernel corn may be substituted.*

4 cooked green mealies or sweetcorn
2 eggs, separated
100 ml cake flour
2 ml baking powder
1 ml salt
grated nutmeg
milled black pepper

Cut the kernels from the corn and chop coarsely (by hand or
in a food processor). Mix in the egg yolks. Sift in the flour
and baking powder, season with salt, nutmeg and pepper
and mix well. Beat the egg white until stiff, and fold in.

Fry spoonfuls in oil in a frying pan over medium heat, until
crisp on both sides. Take care: if insufficiently cooked the
fritters will be runny in the middle. Drain very well on
kitchen paper laid on newspaper, then arrange on a warm
plate. Serve warm.
MAKES ABOUT 12

SPINACH PASTA
WITH CHILLIES AND PEANUTS

*Pasta is relatively new to the South African table
(other than in Italian homes and restaurants), but it is used more
and more often, on its own or as an accompaniment to meat.*

400 g green tagiatelle or fettucine
olive oil
1 bunch spinach, washed and finely shredded
1-2 green or red chillies, finely sliced
and seeded
100 g roasted peanuts, chopped

Bring plenty of salted water to the boil and cook the pasta
until done 'al dente'. Drain. Heat a little olive oil in a frying
pan and fry the spinach, chilli and chopped peanuts until
sizzling hot. Toss in the pasta and serve immediately.
SERVES 4

BRAISED MALAY RICE WITH PEAS

500 ml rice
butter, vegetable oil
1 large onion, chopped
5 ml cumin seeds
3 cardamom pods
2 cassia sticks, or 1 stick cinnamon
2 ml ground allspice
3 whole cloves
10 ml salt
1 litre water
500 ml peas

Heat a little butter and oil in a medium saucepan and fry
the onion until golden. Add the cumin, cardamom, cassia or
cinnamon, allspice and cloves, and sizzle for about 30 seconds. Stir in the rice, then add the salt and water. Cover and
cook gently until the moisture has been absorbed and the
rice is cooked. Stir in the peas and heat through.
SERVES 6-8

SPINACH WITH COURGETTES
AND SLIVERED BILTONG

*This modern recipe reflects a merging of complimentary and
contrasting flavours. When selecting biltong, choose a stick that is
still slightly wet - the colour and texture is better.*

1 bunch spinach, well washed
4 medium courgettes
butter
salt, milled black pepper, grated nutmeg
100 g biltong, finely sliced

Lightly drain the spinach, trim stems and tear leaves into
small pieces. Slice the courgettes lengthwise into fine rib-
bons with a potato peeler.

Heat the butter in a wide saucepan and fry the courgette
until tender. Add the spinach. Cover and steam gently for a
few minutes – it should not be too limp. Remove from the
heat, season with salt, pepper and nutmeg and toss in the
biltong. Serve immediately.
SERVES 4

CARROTS WITH GARLIC AND HERBS

600 g small carrots, scrubbed and trimmed
3-4 sprigs fresh thyme
1 sprig fresh rosemary
30 ml olive oil
12 cloves garlic, halved
salt, milled black pepper

Leave carrots whole or, if they are on the large side, slice fairly thickly on the diagonal. Strip thyme and rosemary leaves from stems. Heat the oil in a non-stick frying pan and lightly brown carrots and garlic over gentle heat, stirring occasionally. Season with salt and pepper, add the herbs and cook for a few minutes more until carrots are tender but still crunchy. Transfer to a warm serving bowl and garnish with extra fresh herbs.
SERVES 4

YELLOW RICE

Geelrys (yellow rice) is great with bobotie and curry. Its other name, begrafnisrys (funeral rice) comes from the fact that it was always part of the meal served after funerals, a tradition of both the Dutch and the Cape Malays.

250 ml rice
60 ml seedless raisins
6 whole cloves
5 ml salt
2 ml turmeric
1-2 thin slices green ginger
625 ml cold water
30 g (30 ml) butter

Combine the rice, raisins, cloves, salt, turmeric, ginger and water in a medium saucepan. Cover and simmer gently until the rice is tender and all the liquid has been absorbed. Add the butter, fluff up with a fork and discard the ginger. Tip into a warm bowl and serve hot.
SERVES 8

GLAZED CARROTS

Our grandmothers mashed carrots and potatoes with butter, milk and a touch of mace or nutmeg. For posher occasions, egg yolks were added and whipped egg white folded in to make a light soufflé. Sweet, glazed carrots are even more popular.

2 bunches carrots, peeled or scraped
125 ml water
150 g butter, cut into small cubes
80 ml honey or brown sugar
5-6 thin slices green ginger
2 ml grated nutmeg
lemon juice

Slice carrots finely. Heat the water in a wide saucepan, add the carrots, butter, honey, ginger, nutmeg and a squeeze of lemon juice. Cover and cook very gently for 5-8 minutes until carrots are almost done. Uncover, increase the heat and continue cooking until the sauce has reduced to a glaze. Discard ginger; serve hot.
SERVES 8

71

SPICY MASHED POTATO

*Indian mashed potato; Cape Malays flavour theirs more
simply with grated nutmeg.*

4 large potatoes, peeled and diced
(about 600 g)
salt
100 g Ghee (page 216), or butter
4-5 cardamom pods, lightly crushed
2 onions, finely sliced
1 small green chilli, finely sliced
and seeded,
or 2 ml Green Masala (page 217)
15 ml lemon juice
small bunch fresh coriander leaves,
well washed, dried and chopped

Cook the potatoes in salted water. Drain most of the liquid
and mash with half the ghee or butter. (If it's too stiff, add a
little milk.)

Heat the remaining ghee or butter in a frying pan, add the
cardamom, then the onion and fry until deep golden brown.
Add the chilli or green masala, mix in the mashed potato
and lemon juice and heat through. Mix in the coriander just
before serving. Serve hot.
SERVES 5-6

CHILLI AND GARLIC POTATO

*Vary the heat factor of this Indian dish by
adjusting the amount of chilli. For quicker
preparation, par-cook the potatoes. Garnish with
coriander leaves if you wish.*

100 g Ghee (page 216), or butter
750 g new potatoes, lightly scrubbed
2 large onions, thickly sliced
3-4 cloves garlic, cut into fine slivers (optional)
1-2 red or green chillies, sliced and seeded
salt, milled black pepper, lemon juice
10 ml cumin seeds, roasted in a dry frying pan

Heat the ghee or butter in a wide frying pan, add the potato, onion, garlic and chilli, and fry until golden. Season with
salt and pepper, cover and cook at a more gentle pace until
vegetables are cooked and well browned.

Add a squeeze of lemon juice, tip into a warm bowl and
garnish with cumin seeds.
SERVES 6

GLAZED SWEET POTATO

*'Patat' satisfies our predilection for something
sweet with our meat. Before sugar was available, honey
was the sweetener, and sheep's tail fat used instead of butter.
Karoo cooks prepare wild kambro (a potato-like tuber
weighing up to 10 kg) this way too.
The entire dish may be baked in the oven, and will
take about 50 minutes in a moderate oven.
Cook covered for part of the time, and uncovered towards
the end to brown the surface.*

1 kg sweet potatoes, peeled
and cubed
125 ml water
1-2 sticks cinnamon
1 piece Dried Naartjie Peel (page 218),
or a few strips of orange rind
100 g butter
125 ml brown sugar
2 thin slices green ginger, or
1 ml dried ginger
60 ml medium sherry

Preheat the oven griller. Combine the sweet potato, water,
cinnamon, naartjie peel or orange rind, butter, sugar and
ginger in a saucepan. Cover and simmer for about 10 minutes until almost tender. Uncover and cook more briskly
until the sweet potato is glazed and most of the liquid has
been absorbed. Shake the pot from time to time to prevent
the sweet potato from burning.

Transfer the sweet potato to a warm bowl, pour over the
sherry and lightly brown under the oven griller.
SERVES 6

BEETROOT WITH A TANGY SAUCE

*This olden-day traditional recipe emanates from
the Free State heartland.*

8 medium beetroot (about 600 g), washed
80 ml wine vinegar
80 ml water
10 ml cornflour
125 ml brown sugar
salt, milled black pepper
50 g butter

Set the oven at 150°C. Cut off the beetroot leaves, leaving a little of the stem intact. Place in a large ovenproof dish and cover with foil, moulding it closely to avoid evaporation of moisture. Bake for about 2 hours until tender. To check, wrinkle the skin near the root; if it comes away easily, the beetroot are cooked. Allow to cool, then skin and cube.

Mix together the vinegar, water and cornflour, pour into a medium saucepan and add the sugar. Bring to the boil, stirring constantly, until thickened. Season with salt and pepper, add the beetroot and butter and simmer until heated through. Transfer to a warm serving bowl.

SERVES 4

SALADS, GRAINS & VEGETABLES

CAULIFLOWER CHEESE

1 medium cauliflower

(about 700 g)

salt

750 ml milk

1 small onion, skinned

1 bay leaf

2 whole cloves

3 black peppercorns

50 g butter

60 ml cake flour

2 ml dry English mustard

100 g Cheddar cheese, grated

125 ml fresh white breadcrumbs

Leave the cauliflower whole or cut into florets. Soak in cold water for a while, then drain. Cook, covered, in salted, boiling water, until tender (don't overcook!). Drain and arrange in an oven-to-table casserole. Set the oven at 200°C.

Combine the milk, onion, bay leaf, cloves and peppercorns in a medium saucepan. Cover, bring to the boil and set aside for 10-15 minutes for the flavours to infuse. Strain.

Melt the butter in a clean saucepan, remove from the heat and stir in the flour and mustard. Slowly stir in the hot milk until well blended. Cook, stirring constantly, for 3-4 minutes until the sauce is smooth and thickened. Remove from the heat and stir in half the cheese. Pour over the cauliflower, top with the remaining cheese and crumbs and bake for about 15-20 minutes until the topping is golden and crunchy.

SERVES 6-8

CINNAMON-BAKED PUMPKIN

Pumpkins were grown long before the Cape was colonized,
and rural folk cook it simply – sliced and boiled, pulped,
or cooked with maize kernels, maize meal or beans.
The Dutch predilection of adding butter and sugar, as reflected in
their earliest written recipes, is a popular habit that still lives on
in modern kitchens. One way was to mash butter, salt, sugar,
cinnamon, and flour and water into cooking pumpkin.
This recipe results in an altogether more appealing dish, as
pumpkin-tips are crisped at the end of the cooking. The oven
temperature and cooking time aren't that crucial,
as pumpkin is normally baked at the same time as meat.
Leftovers whip up deliciously into
Pumpkin Fritters (page 191).

1 kg pumpkin, peeled
salt
200 ml water or orange juice
1 stick cinnamon
80 ml brown sugar
100 g butter
45 ml brandy (optional)

Set the oven at 180°C. Cut the pumpkin into slices 5-cm thick, remove pips (reserve for Roasted Pumpkin Pips, see page 38), and cut into cubes. Place in a casserole – make sure it's large enough to expose a lot of pumpkin to the heat to brown it nicely.

Salt lightly, add water or orange juice, crumble in the cinnamon, sprinkle the sugar over, dot with butter and cover with the lid or foil. Bake for 30 minutes, uncover and cook for a further 30-45 minutes until tender and nicely browned – switch on the oven griller at the end of cooking time if you'd prefer it browner still.

Warm the brandy, flame it and pour over the pumpkin. If time allows, set the dish aside for 30 minutes in the warmer before serving.
SERVES 6

Shahi Paneer (page 76), a delicious, light Indian dish.

PUMPKIN IN SPICED COCONUT

Pumpkin and tomato seem unlikely partners, yet the
combination works exceptionally well.

750 g pumpkin, peeled and pipped
50 g butter
1 large onion, finely sliced
1-2 red or green chillies, sliced and seeded
2 cloves garlic, crushed
2 ml ground cinnamon
1 ml ground nutmeg
1 ml ground ginger
3 large, ripe tomatoes blanched, skinned
and chopped
250 ml coconut cream

Cut the pumpkin into cubes about 1,5 cm in diameter. Heat the butter in a medium saucepan and fry the onion until golden. Stir in the chilli, garlic, cinnamon, nutmeg and ginger, then add the tomato, pumpkin and coconut cream. Cover and simmer gently for about 25 minutes until tender. Uncover and cook briskly until the sauce thickens slightly.
SERVES 6

SHAHI PANEER

This famous Indian dish is made from spiced,
home-made curd cheese. Besides being a sublime vegetarian dish,
it is an unusual side dish to a meat main course.
If you don't wish to make your own paneer (cheese),
substitute ricotta cheese.

2 litres full-cream milk
60 ml lemon juice
45 ml vegetable oil
50 g halved cashew nuts
2 ml cumin seeds
1 large onion, chopped
2-3 green chillies, finely chopped
2 ml salt
2 ml Garam Masala (page 217)
2 ml turmeric
5 ml ground coriander
1 large ripe tomato, sliced
fresh coriander leaves

Bring the milk to the boil in a medium saucepan, add the lemon juice and remove from the heat. Stir until the curds separate from the whey then drain in a colander lined with muslin. (Or use a double layer of 'kitchen wipes'.) Cover and set aside for 1-2 hours for whey to run off.

Squeeze out excess moisture, tip the paneer into a bowl and break up with a fork.

Heat the oil in a frying pan and fry the cashew nuts until golden and aromatic. Remove from the pan and set aside. Add the cumin seeds to the pan, then the onion, and fry over medium heat until translucent.

Add the chilli, salt, garam masala, turmeric and coriander, and fry for 30 seconds. Add the sliced tomato, cover and cook for 2-3 minutes. Add the paneer and heat through. Stir in the nuts and serve hot, garnished with coriander leaves.
SERVES 4

VEGETABLE PILAU

Rice and lentils are the base of this intriguing Indian dish, which
may be served as is (with a couple of sambals, of course), or with
curry. Feel free to add other vegetables of your choice, like finely
slivered carrots, whole kernel corn or green beans, to add colour
and flavour, and to make the dish go further. Use any rice you
fancy – basmati, long-grain or brown.

125 ml brown lentils
375 ml cold water
50 g Ghee (page 216), or butter
4 whole cloves
4 cardamom pods, cracked
1 stick cinnamon
5 ml cumin seeds
2 ml ground turmeric
1 onion, finely chopped
5 ml crushed garlic
2 ml crushed green ginger
5 ml salt
250 ml rice
500 ml boiling water
250 ml peas
1 large onion
flour, salt, vegetable oil
4 hard-boiled eggs, quartered
fresh coriander leaves

Place the lentils in a small saucepan with the cold water. Cover and simmer for 15 minutes. Drain.

Heat the ghee or butter in a medium saucepan. Stir in the cloves, cardamom, cinnamon, cumin and turmeric. Cover and sizzle for 30 seconds. Stir in the onion, garlic, ginger and salt. Cook for 1-2 minutes, then add the rice and boiling water. Cover and simmer until the rice is tender and all the liquid has been absorbed. Add the peas and heat through.

Meanwhile slice the onion and separate into rings. Dust with flour, season with salt and deep fry in hot oil until crisp. Drain well on kitchen paper.

Pile rice on a serving plate and garnish with hot onion rings, hard-boiled eggs and coriander leaves.
SERVES 8-10

DHAL VEGETABLE CURRY

Meat is a luxury in many homes, and housewives are adept at creating wonderful main dishes using only vegetables. Here is a Cape-Malay curry, in which a strong Indian influence is evident.

750 g vegetables: small cauliflower and broccoli
florets, sliced carrot, sliced courgettes
375 ml oil lentils or brown lentils
vegetable oil
2 onions, finely chopped
5-10 ml crushed garlic
1 green chilli, sliced and seeded
2 sticks cassia, or 1 stick cinnamon
3 cardamom pods
15 ml Roasted Masala (page 217)
5 ml ground cumin
5 ml ground coriander
2 ml turmeric
2 ml salt
2 ripe tomatoes, finely chopped
750 ml water

Place lentils in a bowl, cover with plenty of cold water and set aside to soak for 1 hour. Tip off the water and drain well.

Heat a little oil in a large saucepan and fry the onion until golden. Add the garlic, chilli and spices and stir for about 30 seconds. Add the tomato and lentils with 500 ml of the water, cover and simmer gently for about 40 minutes until the lentils are almost tender.

Add the vegetables and remaining water and simmer, covered, for about 20 minutes until cooked. Check the flavour and add a little more salt if necessary. If the curry is too moist, cook uncovered for a few minutes. If it's too dry add a little extra water. Serve with rice and sambals.
SERVES 8

CHAPTER SEVEN
OVERBERG, EASTERN CAPE
& GARDEN ROUTE

ORCHARDS, OYSTERS, NEW FRONTIERS AND FARMLANDS

THE LUSH CAPE WINELANDS give way to the calmer, sun-dappled Overberg and southern coastal areas – a stark colour-contrast to the verdant greenness, but no less dramatic in its unique, monochromatic way.

Travel on to enjoy the heady pleasures of the world-famous (and aptly-named) Garden Route, then explore the historic Eastern Cape 'settler country' where, many years ago, adversity was transformed into opportunity.

The route of white expansion from the fledgling Cape colony during the late seventeenth century established new farmlands and forged new frontiers. Adventurers traversed splendid coastal scenery, encountered wild animals and, on the far eastern border with Transkei, came into conflict with black tribes journeying south. Their mission was similar: to find a settled place of their own. Boer trek-farmers were fleeing British dominance, while black tribesmen were escaping Shaka's uprising in Zululand.

Boers bartered for sheep from resident Hottentots, established stockposts and farms, planted seeds and reaped their crops. The Overberg flourished, ultimately absorbing the Hottentots into farm life. Their successors live on in settled towns bearing names in a long-forgotten language – Kinko, Dipka, Napkei and Kadie – and Christian mission stations at Genadendal and Elim.

The early Overberg encompassed the area beyond the 'mountains of Africa', including Hangklip *tot waar de macht der Hoog Edele Compagnie eindigt*, or, translated from high Dutch, that no-one could be certain where the region

Contented cows in the lush farmlands near Plettenberg Bay, at the heart of the Garden Route.

ABOVE *A horse-drawn buggy takes farmworkers to town through the Bredasdorp strandveld.*
RIGHT *A pristine fisherman's cottage at Waenhuiskrans village, known locally as Arniston.*

ended. As new districts came into being, the concept of 'over the mountain' faded, though never quite disappeared. Today the Overberg encompasses the space between the Riviersonderend and Langeberg mountain ranges, and the sea – areas rich in natural resources and places of cultural and historical interest. The characterful hamlet of Swellendam – South Africa's third oldest town – for example, had an outspan at the Drostdy where horses were rested and travellers purchased live chickens, fresh vegetables and fruit, and 'wheaten bread'. Nowadays a fascinating museum has been created on the site. Flour is still ground here, the machinery powered by an ancient watermill, as it was in the eighteenth century.

In valleys in the mountains behind the town grow a profusion of boysenberries and youngberries. Much of the crop is canned for export and turned into juice and delicious jam, but lots of lovely, ripe berries find their way into farmstalls and onto menus of restaurants in the area.

Now, as in past times, Overberg farmers holiday at the seafood-rich southern coast, in quaint seaside towns such as Gansbaai, Onrust, Struisbaai, Waenhuiskrans (Arniston), Agulhas – the southernmost tip of the African continent – and Hermanus on Walker Bay. This is the heart of the whale route, which attracts visitors from all over the world to watch giants of the deep mate, calve and rear their young between May and November each year.

This southern Cape coast is the centre of the perlemoen (abalone) industry, the smallest in the fishing sector, but one with huge commercial significance, as most of the annual quota is snaffled up by countries in the Far East. South Africans have been partial to this delicious (though toughish) univalve since the earliest times. Strandlopers introduced perlemon to European settlers, who laid the foundations of many of the recipes still used today – including mincing and stewing it slowly in butter, roasting slices in the belly of freshly-cut kelp buried in the coals, and frying steaks in a coating of crumbs.

Linking the Overberg to the Eastern Cape is the Garden Route, 'Eden of the Cape', a picture-perfect melding of lush forests, peaceful lakes and rivers, sandy beaches, placid farmlands, mighty mountain ranges and the azure Indian Ocean. Friendly towns tempt you to linger awhile, and local menus include toothsome regional specialities like Knysna oysters, plump East Coast soles and squid (calamari).

In the early 1600s sailors were reportedly plucking mussels from the rocks at Mossel Bay. Other seafarers stopped by and, after Pedro Alvares Cabral placed a report of his voyage in the trunk of an old milkwood tree for collection by another ship returning to Europe, Mossel Bay became our first post office. Thereafter sailors regularly left mail in the same spot. True to its seafaring past, the bay is home to an extensive fishing fleet.

Inland from the Langeberg (long mountains) and Outeniquas running parallel to the coast comes ostrich meat, which tourists find a particularly interesting alternative to seafood. Outeniqua is Hottentot for 'a man laden

ABOVE *Workers of the Knysna Oyster Company carefully tend oyster beds in the calm waters of the lagoon.*
OPPOSITE *Sea mists envelope Wilderness, one of the most spectacular beaches in the world.*

with honey', and refers to bee-keeping, which was recorded in the area as long ago as 1782. Honey was the only sweetener early Africans knew, for sugar was not yet cultivated.

Knysna, named from the Khoikhoi word meaning 'straight down' (an accurate description of the sheer cliffs of the Heads that protect the lagoon from the open sea) straddles a natural lagoon where some 200 species of fish have been recorded, including the strange, rare sea-horse. Also sheltered in the calm waters are Knysna oysters, the Garden Route's acclaimed gourmet delicacy. Oysters have been raised for 2000 years, and grow wild in many parts of the country, including Algoa Bay further north, Cape Infanta at the mouth of the Breede River to the south, as well as on the West Coast and KwaZulu-Natal.

Early morning in Kleinmond on Sandown Bay, where an Overberg fisherman tries his luck on wave-dashed rocks, accompanied by his trusty hound.

Just as climate and soil influence the characteristics of wine, so water affects the appearance, texture and flavour of oysters. Establishing the Knysna oyster beds in 1948 pioneered aquaculture in this country and, to the delight of local and international aficionados, today oysters are a highlight of menus countrywide.

Despite the charms of the Garden Route, it is not in the nature of pioneers to settle indefinitely. Frontiers everywhere conjure up images of confrontation, and history loves to record tales of bravery, hardship and man's triumph over adversity. The Eastern Cape typifies the vision, starting from a flashpoint of conflict, through many turbulent years, to a conclusion of prosperity and a settled society.

Border clashes between trek-farmers and Xhosas resulted in many boers opting for safer republics further north. To protect the frontier, Britain brought out 1000 men and 300 women to start a new life in an unfamiliar country. The 1820 Settlers, as they are known, were allocated farms, but knew

little about agriculture. To make matters worse, the land was unsuitable for farming – trek-farmers called it Zuurveld (sour land), and with good cause. Wheat crops failed, and Xhosa raids continued, forcing many new settlers to move to villages and ultimately to scatter throughout the country.

Some stayed, however, spurred on by initial agricultural failures to move in new directions. Merino sheep were imported from Britain to replace the fat-tailed sheep that had long been farmed here. Merinos, however, preferred the dry Karoo, and the sheep and wool industry shifted there and flourished. Other crops, like oranges and chicory, a coffee additive, were established.

Bathurst, a minuscule town, once the administrative centre for the 1820 Settlers – became the heart of a thriving pineapple industry, which had humble beginnings in a Grahamstown barber shop. Farmer Charles Purdon spotted jars of pineapples rooting in water. He took a few home to plant and the delicious fruit flourished. Today, although much of the crop is canned for the export market, a great deal still finds its way onto local menus, and may be purchased at farmstalls and from hawkers.

Grahamstown has other fascinating stories to tell. Founded in 1812 as a military outpost, it is the best preserved Victorian city in South Africa, and has grown into an important educational and cultural centre. It is the home of the annual Festival of the Arts.

Cities like East London and Port Elizabeth, gateway for the 1820 Settlers, form business and holiday bases. Many once tumbledown Eastern Cape settler homes have been meticulously renovated and preserved, some delightfully transformed into pubs and cosy country hotels. Game reserves have been established, their mission being to

ABOVE LEFT *The Cock House, an historical guest house and restaurant in Grahamstown.*

TOP *Fishing boats return from sea in the rays of the setting sun.*

BOTTOM *Tiny pineapples grow to maturity in the lush soil of plantations near Bathurst.*

restock indigenous animals and protect them for the benefit of future generations.

It is a special pleasure to see the herds multiplying and running free, to dine in characterful restaurants serving local specialities, and to sleep in rooms where early settlers dreamed of peace and posterity.

CHAPTER EIGHT
FISH & SHELLFISH

THE OCEAN IS SOUTHERN Africa's historical gateway, and our symbiosis with the sea starts with our respect for it, extends to our skill as fishermen, and comes full circle with our enjoyment of all seafood.

Creatures which swim, crawl and cling to wave-washed rocks have been caught, and prepared by skilful cooks of every creed, colour and religion since the beginning of time. Examination of ancient middens and relics of primitive fish traps prove that Strandlopers were masters of the art of ferreting out nourishment from the sea. However, due to the similarity between fish and snakes, seafood is not part of the traditional black diet, though some coastal-dwellers like the Tsonga and Xhosa people trap and spear fish to eat, and women collect shellfish, and shells are used for spoons and pot scrapers.

Most of the Dutch fish names were bestowed by Jan van Riebeeck, whose soldiers were fed so much fish there was once talk of mutiny! The Governor's response was to extend the rations to include the meat and eggs of penguins and other seabirds.

Fishing skills had to be learnt, however, as Europeans were relatively ignorant in this regard. But no sooner had they mastered the art, and experienced the delights of such fishy feasts as perlemoen (abalone), alikreukels and mussels, their passion grew and, for most creatures of the sea remains undiminished to this day.

Some creatures – octopus, sea urchins, periwinkles, limpets and the like – never featured prominently on the Cape table, though a rich soup was made by scrubbing and soaking limpets in fresh water, then crushing (shells and all) and simmering in water together with onions, garlic, seaweed and peppercorns. The strained broth was thickened with flour and water, and finished with a dash of sherry.

LEFT *Ingredients for Fish Stock (page 216).*
ABOVE *Pickled Fish (page 93).*

Though palatable, octopus and redbait were most often used as bait, as was chokka (squid, also known as calamari), prolific in eastern Cape waters, which is exported in huge quantities, and snaffled up by local restaurants for crumbing and deep-frying, or sizzling in garlic butter.

Fish became a source of Government revenue in the late 1700s. Steam-driven trawlers sailed from Simon's Town and other coastal places. On their return fresh fish would be laid out on the sand and sold by the bunch to Cape Malay ven-

dors, who slung fish-filled baskets on bamboo yokes over their shoulders, and peddled their wares from door to door. At the sound of their fish horns, kitchen maids and cooks would come to purchase fresh fish.

Horns were first made of hollow kelp found washed up on the beach; later they were fashioned from paraffin tins, while fish carts replaced foot-slogging vendors. Sadly, with the advent of modern supermarkets, the vendors and the call of the horn have been silenced forever.

FRIED FISH WITH TARTARE SAUCE

Simple recipes are best for all kinds of fish, especially if it's fresh from the sea. In times past, frying was done in lard or sheep's tail fat; butter mixed with oil is a far healthier option. Maize meal replaces the more common breadcrumbs or batter coating. Tartare sauce may be refrigerated for up to five days.

750 g filleted fish (skin on or off)
salt, milled black pepper
1 egg, lightly beaten
maize meal, butter, vegetable oil
TARTARE SAUCE
250 ml Mayonnaise (page 218)
2 hard-boiled eggs, finely chopped
7 ml Dijon mustard
15 ml chopped fresh parsley
15 ml snipped chives
15 ml capers or chopped gherkin

TARTARE SAUCE Mix the ingredients together and check the flavour, adding a touch of salt and pepper or lemon juice if you wish. Spoon into a serving bowl, cover and chill.

Cut the fish into serving portions and season with salt and pepper. Dip in egg and coat lightly with maize meal. Heat a generous amount of butter and oil in a large, non-stick frying pan. As it starts to brown, add two portions of fish. Fry until sealed, then lift the fish and swish the pan with buttery oil. Cook fish until beautifully browned.

Turn fish, reduce the heat and cook through over gentle heat. The cooking time will vary depending on the thickness and texture of the fish, but the whole procedure should only take a few minutes.

Drain fish, place on warm serving plates and keep hot. Add more butter and oil to the pan and fry remaining fish in the same way. Serve with crisp chips and tartare sauce.
SERVES 4

Fried Fish with Tartare Sauce and chips is served for lunch in the shady gardens at Cybele Forest Lodge, near White River in Mpumalanga.

FRIED HARDERS

When trek fishermen haul their catch of wriggling harders onto the beach, this is most often the way they are cooked – with minimum effort. Mullet and sardines may be done this way too.

fresh harders
coarse salt
Ghee (page 216), or butter and vegetable oil

Vlek (butterfly) the fish by cutting through the backbone to hinge open at the belly. Clean well, rinse and place skin down – still dripping wet – on a tray. Cover completely with coarse salt (don't substitute fine salt). Set aside for 30 minutes, then rinse off the salt under cold running water.

Peg fish onto the washing line and allow to wind-dry for 4-6 hours until they become firm to the touch. Fry in sizzling ghee, or butter and oil until crisp and golden. Serve with lemon wedges for squeezing.

SMOORVIS

'Smothered fish' was originally prepared with fish which had been salted and dried in sea breezes. After soaking in water, the flesh was flaked and 'smoored' in spicy rice. Smoked fish is more often used today. Though similar to many highly spiced rice dishes of India, this recipe is attributed to Cape Malays, who have for centuries prepared similar dishes using ingredients as diverse as lobster and hard-boiled penguin eggs, and less exotic fish and chicken eggs. Crabs and mussels were also used. Smoorvis should be pungent and neither too dry nor too moist.
It is delicious with wholewheat bread and atjar.

500 g smoked fish, boned, skinned and
roughly flaked
2 onions, finely sliced
butter, vegetable oil
2 potatoes, peeled and cut into small cubes
5 ml crushed green ginger
1-2 red or green chillies, finely sliced and seeded
2 large, ripe tomatoes blanched, skinned
and chopped
500 ml cooked rice
60 ml sultanas (optional)
salt, milled black pepper, lemon juice

Lightly brown the onion in a little butter and oil in a large frying pan. Add the potato and fry until golden. Stir in the ginger, chilli and tomato, and cook over very gentle heat for a few minutes more. Stir occasionally.

Mix in the fish, rice and sultanas. Cover and steam over low heat until piping hot and the potato is cooked. Flavour with pepper, and a little salt if necessary.

Tip smoorvis into a warm serving dish, and add a good squeeze of lemon juice.
SERVES 4

FISH BOBOTIE

*Thank Mr Henry Cloete, owner of the
historic Alphen estate in the Constantia valley, for this
unique baked fish 'pudding'. Over a century ago, bored with
bobotie made from left-over mutton, he asked his cook to
make a fish variation instead. Any white fish may be used
(old manuscripts suggest adding a few oysters as well),
and a few tablespoons of sultanas or seedless raisins,
or chopped dried apricots or peaches plumped in boiling water,
for sweetness. Fish bobotie is delicious for breakfast, lunch or
supper. It is best served straight from the oven, though it may be
prepared – prior to cooking – a day ahead and kept chilled.
Don't add the custard topping until just before it
goes into the oven.*

750 g skinless fish fillets
2 slices day-old white bread (crusts on)
250 ml milk
1 egg, lightly beaten
finely grated rind and juice of 1 small lemon
5 ml salt, milled black pepper
butter
1 large onion, finely chopped
1 red chilli, sliced, seeded and finely chopped
10 ml fish masala or curry powder
12 lemon leaves
12 almonds
TOPPING
2 eggs
125 ml milk
2 ml salt, white pepper

Set the oven at 180°C. Butter a 2-litre oven-to-table casserole. Mince or finely chop the fish. Crumb the bread, pour the milk over and gently stir in the egg, lemon rind and juice, salt and pepper.

Heat the butter in a frying pan, add the onion and chilli and fry until golden. Sprinkle in the masala or curry powder and cook for 30 seconds. Remove from the heat and mix in the fish and crumbs. Spoon into the baking dish and smooth the surface. Roll the lemon leaves and bury them in the bobotie, interspersed with almonds.

Mix the topping eggs, milk, salt and pepper and pour over. Cover with foil or the lid and place casserole in a larger baking dish. Add boiling water to come halfway up the sides and bake for 40 minutes. Uncover for the final 15 minutes to lightly brown and set the topping. Serve with rice and sambals.
SERVES 6

FISH CAKES

*Fish cakes (or fish frikkadelle) may be flavoured in different
ways and served at any meal of the day – even as cocktail
snacks impaled on toothpicks.
Indian cooks perk them up with spices, while Cape Malays
replace mashed potato with breadcrumbs soaked in water,
and occasionally add finely chopped tomato to the mixture.
Old recipes advocate the addition of butter or cream, as well as
finely chopped almonds and chutney.
Any type of fish will do, either left-over or freshly cooked
for the occasion.*

500 g cooked fish fillets
300 g potatoes, peeled and cubed
salt, milled black pepper
60 ml grated onion
45 ml chopped fresh parsley
1 ml grated nutmeg
2 eggs, lightly beaten
toasted crumbs

Skin and flake the fish. Cook the potato in a little salted boiling water. Drain, mash and season with salt and pepper. Mix in the fish, onion, parsley, nutmeg and beaten egg.

Drop spoonfuls into the crumbs and coat evenly. Form into balls or patties, and flatten slightly. Fry fish cakes in hot oil until crisp and golden. Drain on kitchen paper. Serve hot or cool with a sauce of your choice.

INDIAN FISH CAKES Add to the mixture 125 ml chopped fresh coriander leaves, 2 ml fish masala or Green Masala (page 217), 2 ml ground turmeric, and a generous squeeze of lemon juice.
MAKES ABOUT 16

PENANG FISH

This age-old recipe may be prepared with any type of fish.

750 g filleted, skinless fish

50 g dried tamarind seed

Ghee (page 216), or butter

2 onions, finely sliced

10 ml curry powder

2 ml crushed garlic

1 ml ground ginger

15 ml lemon juice

salt

250 ml coconut cream

250 ml Fish Stock (page 216)

Cut the fish into steaks. Soak the tamarind in a little hot water for about 30 minutes. Strain and discard the seed.

Heat a little butter in a wide frying pan. Add the onion and fry until deep golden brown. Stir in the curry powder, garlic, ginger, lemon juice and tamarind, and season with salt.

Pour in the coconut cream and fish stock, and bring to the boil. Add the fish and simmer, uncovered, for about 5 minutes until cooked. Serve hot with rice or potatoes, and atjar.

▲ SERVES 4

▲

Smoked Fish prepared with freshly caught yellowtail.

MASALA FISH

This Eastern dish – similarly recorded by both Indian and Cape-Malay food writers – is great, whatever fish you use.

750 g filleted fish (skin on or off)

10 ml ground cumin

10 ml ground coriander

5 ml crushed garlic

1-2 green chillies, finely chopped

2 ml salt

5 ml turmeric

30 ml vegetable oil

15 ml lemon juice

Cut the fish into serving portions. Mix together the remaining ingredients to a form a paste, rub into the fish and set aside for about 1 hour. (Or cover and chill for up to 5 hours.)

Fry in hot vegetable oil until done; about 4-5 minutes on each side. Serve with atjar, and lemon wedges for squeezing.

SERVES 6-8

SMOKED FISH

Smoking, salting and drying have been used to preserve fish for centuries, and smoked fish fresh from smoking ovens is popular with visitors to open-air restaurants around our coastline. Many old-timers still smoke their fish in 20-gallon metal drums; modern home-smokers are much easier to use. Any type of fish may be smoked, but make sure it's of suitable dimensions to fit into the smoker. If possible, serve soon after smoking – after it has cooled. Left-overs make wonderful smoorvis (page 90).

1 whole, fresh fish
sea salt or coarse salt
fresh herbs, lemon wedges

Wash, scale, gut and behead the fish. Cut one fillet from the bone; leave the other attached, with the skin on. Lay flat on the rack of the smoker.

Sprinkle sea salt or coarse salt over. Firm, flavourful fish such as snoek, angelfish and yellowtail need to be more heavily salted than delicately flavoured types like kob or salmon trout. Place fish in a cool spot for an hour or two, rinse and salt lightly again.

Sprinkle about 60 ml oak sawdust on smoker base, arrange the rack (with the fish) in the smoker box and cover with the lid. Place over medium heat (either the coals of a fire or a gas burner) until the sawdust burns. This creates the smoke to cook the fish. Watch carefully; if things get too hot it will cause a bitter flavour. After 15-20 minutes your fish should be cooked. Test to see if the flesh flakes easily.

Place the fish on a tray, garnish with herbs and serve with lemon wedges for squeezing and a complementary sauce.

PICKLED FISH

In the early 1800s the Green Point common on the outskirts of Cape Town was a racecourse, where folk met twice a year for a day of sport and culinary delights such as suckling pig, braaied snoek, watermelon konfyt and pickled fish. This recipe was devised by Cape Malays, expert fishermen, who are incredibly adept at preserving their catch to make it last as long as possible. The recipe eloquently highlights the impact that Eastern influences had on local cuisine. Generations of housewives have taken advantage of the summer's gamefish-run to pickle fish in bulk and store it for the coming months. Firm-fleshed snoek and yellowtail are favoured, but any other fish may be substituted – even humble hake. If purchasing a whole fish to fillet, choose one of 2,5-3 kg. Frying fish before pickling is the traditional way, but you may bake or microwave it if you prefer.

1,7-2 kg filleted fish, skinned
vegetable oil
750 ml grape vinegar
250 ml water
200 ml sugar
15 ml turmeric
30 ml curry powder
7 ml salt
15 ml black peppercorns
15 ml coriander seeds
4 large onions, finely sliced
6 lemon or bay leaves
2 green or red chillies, sliced and seeded
4 thin slices green ginger
45 ml cake flour
250 ml sultanas (optional)

Cut the fish into 3-cm cubes. Fry in hot oil until cooked through; drain well on kitchen paper.

Combine the vinegar, water, sugar, turmeric, curry powder, salt, peppercorns and coriander seeds in a large saucepan and bring to the boil. Add the onions, lemon or bay leaves, chillies and ginger, cover and simmer for 10-12 minutes. The onion should be limp but still slightly crunchy. Drain the pickling mixture into a clean saucepan (reserve the onion) and bring to the boil. Mix a little sauce into the flour to form a thin paste, stir into the sauce and simmer for about 2 minutes to thicken slightly.

Layer fish, sultanas and onion in a large glass dish, pour over the sauce, cover and refrigerate. Pickled fish may be eaten as soon as it cools down; however the flavour is even better after a couple of days. Firm fish will keep for up to 6 months in the fridge; delicate fish such as hake and kob may be kept for 2-3 months.

SERVES 6-8

TROUT WITH HERBED SPINACH

2 x 300 g whole trout

50 g butter

1 small onion, finely chopped

2 ml crushed garlic

250 g button mushrooms, sliced

1 bunch spinach, washed, drained and shredded
(discard thick ribs)

1 ripe tomato, finely diced

15 ml chopped fresh herbs (parsley, fennel, thyme)

salt, milled black pepper

60 ml lemon juice

200 ml white wine

125 ml cream

Clean the trout thoroughly. Set the oven at 180°C. Heat the butter in a medium saucepan and gently fry the onion, garlic and mushrooms for a few minutes until tender. Add the spinach, tomato, herbs and seasoning, cover and sweat very gently for 5 minutes. Allow to cool.

Fill the trout with the stuffing. Place in a baking dish and add the lemon juice and wine. Season with salt and pepper, cover with foil and bake for about 20 minutes until cooked.

Place fish on warm serving plates. Add the cream to the pan juices and boil, uncovered, on the stove-top until reduced to form a thin sauce. Pour alongside the trout.
SERVES 2

BLACK MUSSELS
IN SAFFRON CURRY SAUCE

This modern version of a classic Cape recipe is a signature dish at the acclaimed Constantia Uitsig restaurant in the heart of the Cape winelands.

36 black mussels, scrubbed clean

400 g puff pastry

1 egg, lightly beaten

6 saffron threads

125 ml warm water

500 ml dry white wine

1 onion, finely chopped

30 ml chopped fresh parsley

5 ml curry powder

125 ml cream

500 g young spinach leaves

butter

200 ml finely chopped tomato

Set the oven at 200°C. Cut the pastry into six triangles. Place on a lightly oiled baking tray and brush with egg. Bake for 15-20 minutes until puffed and golden. While still warm, slit each triangle through the middle.

Soak the saffron in warm water for 30 minutes. Bring the wine to the boil in a large pot with the onion and parsley. Add the mussels, cover and cook over high heat for about 5 minutes until they open. Remove from the pot, discard the shells and pull out the 'beards'.

Add the curry powder to the stock and boil uncovered until reduced by half. Add the cream, and reduce again until the sauce thickens. (It should be strongly flavoured and naturally salted from the mussels). Strain into a clean saucepan and add the saffron.

Blanch the spinach in salted boiling water for 2 minutes. Drain. Just before serving, fry gently in a little butter for about 2 minutes more.

TO SERVE Warm the mussels in the sauce. Put a little spinach on each plate. Place a pastry base on top, spoon on mussels and sauce, cover with pastry tops and garnish with chopped tomato.
SERVES 6

LOBSTER
WITH SHERRY MAYONNAISE

Early cookbooks called rock lobsters kreeft (shortened to kreef),
although modern cooks know them as crayfish.

4 whole lobsters or 8 lobster tails
SHERRY MAYONNAISE
125 ml medium-cream sherry
125 ml thick cream
250 ml Mayonnaise (page 218)
salt, milled black pepper, snipped chives

SHERRY MAYONNAISE Pour the sherry into a small saucepan and boil uncovered until reduced to a thin syrup. Allow to cool then mix with the cream and mayonnaise. Season with salt and pepper. Stir in a few snipped chives.

Drown the lobsters by immersing them in cold, fresh water; this will take about 30 minutes. Weigh them, and cook in a large pot of salted boiling water for 6 minutes per 500 g. Start timing only when the liquid returns to the boil.

Allow to cool then scrub the shells clean in cold water. Cut lobsters in half; devein. Serve with lemon wedges for squeezing and sherry mayonnaise, offered separately.
SERVES 4

4 lobsters
250 ml Fish Stock (page 216)
vegetable oil
12 pickling onions, peeled
10 ml crushed garlic
1-2 fresh chillies, finely sliced
and seeded
4-5 curry leaves
5 ml ground cumin
5 ml ground coriander
2 ml turmeric
1 ml ground cardamom
1 stick cinnamon
4 large, ripe tomatoes blanched, skinned
and chopped
lemon juice
salt, milled black pepper
60 ml plain yoghurt (optional)

LOBSTER CURRY

*Cape Malays were the first to braise lobster in spices, which
resulted in this delicious curry, for which many variations exist.
Earlier writers specify tamarind juice; more recently this has been
replaced by lemon juice. For a simpler recipe, use lobster tails
instead of whole lobsters and omit the first step in the method. If
you like, add a dash of Roasted Masala (page 217) with the
yoghurt at the end of the cooking time.*

Pull the lobsters apart to separate tails from bodies. Wash well. Cut off fanned tail shells; set aside. Pull out the alimentary canal. Slice tails through lengthwise (first snip through the under-shell with scissors).

Bring the fish stock to the boil in a large saucepan, add lobster bodies and tail fans and boil for 6 minutes (no longer or you will overcook the legs). Remove from the pot. Pull off legs and claws, cover and set aside with the tail fans (they will later decorate the completed dish). Strain and retain the stock for the sauce.

Heat a little oil in a large saucepan and lightly cook the lobster tail pieces for about 1 minute. Set aside.

Lightly brown the onions and garlic in the same pot (add extra oil if necessary), then add the chilli, curry leaves, cumin, coriander, turmeric, cardamom and cinnamon. Sizzle the spices for about 30 seconds, then add the chopped tomato, lemon juice, stock and a little salt and pepper. Cover and simmer for about 10 minutes.

Just before serving return the lobster to the sauce and simmer for 2-3 minutes until cooked. Add the yoghurt and heat through. Tip into a warm bowl, or serve directly from the pan. Garnish with the reserved tail fans and legs, and serve with rice and sambals.

SERVES 4

PRAWNS PERI-PERI

Our appreciation of peri-peri prawns comes from Mozambique, where these shellfish are cooked in the traditional Portuguese style.

18-24 large prawns
200 g butter
10 ml crushed garlic
30 ml lemon juice
30 ml peri-peri sauce (recipe below)
salt, milled black pepper
PERI-PERI SAUCE
50 g red chillies, very finely chopped
5 cloves garlic, crushed
500 ml olive oil
pared rind of 1 small lemon

PERI-PERI SAUCE Mix the ingredients together in a bottle and shake well. You can make the sauce ahead and store it in the fridge; the flavour improves with age, reaching its peak at two weeks.

Slit prawns down their backs and devein. Leave heads on, or remove if you prefer. Depending on the size of your frying pan, cook them in one or two batches.

Heat the butter gently and add the garlic and lemon juice. Don't let the garlic burn. Add prawns and peri-peri sauce. (Shake first to make sure you get some of the chilli and garlic as well.)

Sizzle for 4-5 minutes, turning frequently, until cooked. Season with salt and pepper and tip into a warm serving bowl. Garnish, if you wish, with chopped fresh parsley. Serve with rice or bread and butter.

SERVES 3-4

CHAPTER NINE
KAROO
& NORTHERN CAPE

KOPPIES AND CAMPFIRE TALES, OLIVES AND OSTRICHES

OUTSIDE OF ASIA, OUR sunbaked Karoos form the most spacious plateaux in the world, covering one-third South Africa's surface. Flat-topped hillocks – the country's most characteristic scenic emblem – dot the landscape. The air is fresh, the sun sets in an almost indecent flooding of colour, and night skies are lit by pinpricks of a myriad brilliant stars.

Whether passing through, or spending time here away from the frenzied pace of big city life, your perspective of time, distance and the tenacity of man shifts, for it is all but impossible to imagine anyone surviving in such a harsh, unforgiving terrain. Yet these were once rich hunting grounds of the San who, by bonding with their environment, found comfort in its harshness, companionship in its loneliness, and learnt patient resignation from its ruthlessness.

As in many isolated places of the world where man has struggled for survival, food – now as then – is all the more precious for its scarcity, and perfectly reflects a rugged, nomadic lifestyle. Sustenance came from the meat of antelope and larger animals like zebra, elephant, hippo and buffalo. Veldkos included wild bulbs, fruits and berries, roots and tubers and leaves and seeds of bushes. Wild honey was collected; nectar was gathered from red aloes.

When nineteenth-century trek-farmers came they lived off the land as well; kelkiewyn (Namaqua partridges) were simmered in potjies; bredies were prepared with gourds; kambro were made into jam and served as a vegetable. Venison was smoked, or marinated and roasted – dishes far removed from intricate, spice-fragrant Western Cape fare of the time.

Korbeelhuise (corbelled houses) near Williston in the Great Karoo, were built from stone by early trek-farmers.

Ovens for baking bread, puddings, pies, and vegetables such as patat (sweet potato) and pumpkin, were fashioned from hollowed-out ant-heaps. Fruit of the rosyntjiebos (raisin bush) was crushed and made into brandy for an after-dinner soet-soepie (sweet drink).

Karoo food was called skoff (cuisine is far too posh a term) derived from Dutch sailors' *schaften*, or noon meal. Skof is also Afrikaans for stage (or trek), indicating the meal at the end of a journey.

Klein (Little) Karoo plains are cradled in a nest of rugged mountain ranges forming a natural buffer from the coastal terrace. The way in is through kloofs so daunting that it wasn't until 1689 that the first whites managed the journey. The San called the area Kannaland after a wild bush; other

Dennehof Karoo Guest House, in the tiny hamlet of Prince Albert on the cusp of the Great Karoo.

names included 'land of thirst' and 'karo' meaning dry – no understatement when one experiences this seemingly barren yet compelling area.

Small farming communities grow potatoes, figs, olives, apples, pears, peaches and apricots. Brandy is distilled; fine cheeses are prepared. Wines come from the Breede River Valley and towns such as Robertson and Montagu, particularly sweet Muscadel and Muscat d'Alexandrie (known in these parts as Hanepoot).

Worcester, the largest town in the valley, grows grapes and houses many wine co-operatives. Graaff-Reinet, 'the gem of the Karoo', is surrounded by the Karoo Nature Reserve, watched over by Spandau Kop mountain and not far from the Valley of Desolation, which was declared a National Monument in 1938. Aged buildings are lovingly restored to maintain the gracious nineteenth-century atmosphere.

BELOW *Remnants of the San (Bushmen) people have gathered together at Schmitsdrif near Kimberley, where these old-timers make their fire under a canvas canopy.*
BOTTOM *Farm workers in the Little Karoo transport fire-wood in their trusty donkey cart.*

The Cango Valley, 'a place rich in water', famous for the Cango Caves, is a high-lying central plateau, home to the ostrich, an ungainly, foul-tempered oddity of the bird fraternity, which has inhabited the area for a long, long time. San hunters disguised themselves with ostrich skins over their backs and one arm held aloft to resemble the bird's long neck! They ate the eggs (one is equivalent to twenty-four hens' eggs, and takes about an hour to boil). Ostrich eggs make nifty water carriers: take an egg, bore a hole at each end, expel the egg inside the shell; fill with water and close with a makeshift plug! They can be buried in deep sand for retrieval during times of water shortage.

The Oudtshoorn ostrich market peaked in about 1882 when feathers – our fourth most valuable export after gold, diamonds and wool – adorned both showgirls of France and society ladies of America. At home feathers were put to more mundane purposes – dusting homes and waving about during banquets to keep flies at bay! In the 1990s ostrich meat attained international acclaim. Although a red meat similar to beef in taste and texture, ostrich has virtually no fat and contains only a vestige of cholesterol. As a result it is much in demand on the local and international food scene.

Karoo mutton is famous for its succulence and flavour. Flocks of Merinos feast on wild rosemary, Karoo bush, brakbos (similar to saltbush of Australian sheep country), and gannabos. Sheep and mutton feature prominently on menus. Legs are roasted, chops are braaied, shoulders are baked. Chubby tails of the blackhead Persian render rich fat which is excellent for cooking and baking. Bits of crisp, salted fat, called kaaiings (crackling) and toutjiesvleis (string-like biltong strips), are popular snacks.

Earlier specialities include offal chopped up into bobotie and simmered in potjiekos, gullets stuffed with prickly pear, tripe filled with chopped liver, large intestines crisply braaied over the coals, and sausage flavoured with garlic, sage, thyme, coriander, lemon rind and black pepper. Fried offal cakes, known as pannas, were prepared with tripe and trotters spiced with cloves, nutmeg, coriander and black pepper.

Prickly pears proliferate throughout the Little Karoo. The plants were introduced from South America to form protective hedges around early Cape homesteads. During the 1930s the fruit was hawked by farm workers to townsfolk, who made preserves, syrup and atjar from the leaves, and

Many Karoo folk are as nomadic as their forebears were. Farm labourers in the Great Karoo pack their treasured possessions on rickety carts and take to the road in search of seasonal work.

brewed heady beer. The plants multiplied, thereby destroying vast tracts of grazing land. Mechanical eradication and moths brought from Argentina failed to curb the spread; eventually cochineal insects weakened plants sufficiently to allow them to be felled.

The semi-desert Great Karoo abuts the Little Karoo and is bordered by southern mountain ranges – the Hex River, Swartberg, Baviaanskloof, Great Winterhoek and Suurberg. In the west is Namaqualand and the Cederberg and Lower Bokkeveld. The Orange River borders the northern boundary. Southerly-migrating Hottentots named the plains garob – dry, unfruitful, uninhabited, rolled into one.

Farmers in the Williston-Fraserburg-Carnarvon triangle lived in korbeelhuise (corbelled houses), built entirely from flat rocks, as wood was unobtainable in the area. They were

cool in summer and warm in winter, for fires were lit inside and a flat stone at the apex of the domed roof was pushed aside to serve as a chimney.

Take time to explore the Northern Cape rather than taking the lickety-split road from the Cape to Gauteng via Kimberley or Bloemfontein. Encircled by the dust-dry upper Karoo, southern Kalahari and Namaqualand highlands, the visual splendour comes as a delightful surprise, for here you will find a thriving farming community in the lush Orange River Valley. A river – the Khoikhoi's !Garib, (great river) – runs through rust-red, rolling sand dunes. After rising some 2000 kilometres away in Lesotho, it crashes grandly into the Augrabies gorge near Upington, then flows on to form South Africa's boundary with Namibia on its journey to the Atlantic Ocean.

River banks are lined with date palms, pomegranate trees, orange groves, fruit orchards, vegetable patches, and fields of cotton and lucerne. Vineyards are plentiful, the fruit destined for drying and the wine co-op. Some of the first hand-built irrigation canals still zigzag through the countryside – evidence of earlier farmers who looked to the future.

Kalahari truffles, one of Africa's most unusual delicacies, are indigenous to the Northern Cape. Located in the red desert sands around the thorny acacia bush, they grow in deep desert cracks, a few centimetres under the soil, or several metres underground. Some are the size of one's thumb; others as large as an apple. Goats and dogs ferret them out, in the same fashion that truffle-snuffling pigs and dogs do it in more sophisticated areas of Europe. Simply steamed and seasoned, truffles are insipid, but their fragrance is a wonderful flavour-enhancer when partnered with other ingredients.

The visual splendour and culinary diversity of the Karoos and Northern Cape proves that South Africa is, indeed, a land of contrasts, contradictions and incongruity. The region appeals to those who heed the call of relative solitude – keen to forsake urban stress for rural bliss, to enjoy the stark beauty of sunbaked plains, and to revel in the serenity of having space to spare, and to hear campfire tales that revolve around half-remembered times.

Homely bed-and-breakfast establishments and guest houses are to be found in revamped farmhouses. There are stoeps to lounge on, open fireplaces to ward off winter's chill, and high-ceilinged rooms to alleviate the heat of summer.

Even though plains no longer thunder with the hooves of countless antelope, areas once grazed by sheep almost to the point of no return are being gradually restocked with game. Though veldkos is becoming scarcer, and skills required in

ABOVE *A basketful of ostrich eggs.*
RIGHT *Prickly pears in bloom in the Little Karoo.*
OPPOSITE *Baby ostriches huddle together on a farm near Oudtshoorn in the Little Karoo.*

its preparation are dying out, those who know where to find it gather it wisely and prepare it well. You may still find kambro (a potato-like tuber) – traditionally flavoured with ginger, wild fennel and honey – on menus in dusty towns.

Important things are still held dear by folk whose roots run deep. The same simple foods that sustained hunter-gatherers and trek-farmers – a culinary legacy their descendants still hold dear – are faithfully prepared from traditional recipes. If home is, as they say, where the heart is, homely, hearty Karoo skoff will be around a while longer.

CHAPTER TEN
POULTRY, MEAT, OFFAL & GAME

THE AFRICAN SAVANNAH ONCE thundered with the hoofs of plains' game, a rich source of food for all her people. Hunters bagged antelope, lion, elephant, rhinoceros and hippo, and smaller animals like jackal, ostrich, hare, hedgehog and mouse. Wild birds, locusts, flying ants, termites, caterpillars (including the highly prized mopane worm), sand crickets and beetles were hugely enjoyed.

Settlers learned hunting skills from residents of the land they now called home, for in Europe hunting – for larger game at least – was the prerogative of the nobility. Even so, providing sufficient fresh meat for ships visiting the Cape of Good Hope was a problem.

LEFT *Rack of Lamb with Roasted Vegetables (page 112), photographed at Claridge Wine estate in the Wellington hills, Boland.*
ABOVE *Herb-crusted Venison with Rosemary (page 125).*

The long sea journey hampered the importing of breeding stock and, as neither Strandlopers nor San owned sheep or cattle, meat was bartered from Hottentots to the north.

Dassies, seagulls and penguins (and their eggs) appeared on the Cape table. Later pigs were imported and hares and sheep were bred. Prior to refrigeration, pickling vats were always full. Tassal meat – tender strips of a pig or buck – were seasoned with salt and roasted coriander and covered with vinegar, and could be kept for weeks, before being rinsed and fried.

Joints of mutton or venison were larded with bacon, steeped in vinegar flavoured with cloves, lemon leaves, thyme, peppercorns and coriander, then rubbed with flour, topped with lard and roasted. Modern cooks seldom marinate venison and avoid the addition of lard, though studding with bacon still imparts essential succulence and flavour.

Meat is viewed differently in various cultures, and, as a result, it is here that we find the strongest evidence of our rich and diverse heritage. In tribal communities, for example, cooking methods are simplest – boiling or roasting over the fire – and strict religious and ancestral customs dictate both slaughtering and portioning. Cape Malays, on the other hand, employ a myriad spices in their recipes, and follow the teachings of Islam, which dictates which food may and may not be eaten. Cape-Dutch recipes are plainer, and call for an abundance of fat or butter.

Though never considered a status food, offal (or afvalkos) has always been popular on South African menus, both at home and at restaurants. The French Huguenots, particularly partial to offal, fine-tuned offal recipes, influencing the preparation of the meat, and lightening up on both the flavouring and the amount of fat used.

With urbanisation and the gradual taming of the continent, wild meats made way for domesticated livestock – long considered the measure of the status of tribal folk.

Nowadays few men hunt for the pot. However, for times when comfort-zone fare is called for, we enjoy looking over our shoulders to the ways of our forebears.

 Cape-Dutch Chicken Pie (page 109), at the original kitchen of the Boschendal manor house, Cape winelands.

CAPE-DUTCH CHICKEN PIE

Pies were all the rage in Holland in the eighteenth century, a fashion which spread to the Cape. They were also amongst the earliest bakes sold by the 'free bakers' in the colony. Hoenderpastei is associated with celebrations – Christmas, birthdays and especially Cape-Malay wedding feasts. Free-range chickens of days gone by imparted much more flavour than today's battery-reared birds, so this pie deviates slightly in method from the simpler cooking process used by our great-grandmothers.

400 g flaky or puff pastry
1 large chicken
butter
1 large onion, finely chopped
salt, milled black pepper
125 ml dry white wine
250 ml Chicken Stock (page 216)
10 black peppercorns
3 whole cloves
6 whole allspice
30 ml sago
2 egg yolks, lightly beaten
lemon juice
200 g ham, diced
2 hard-boiled eggs, sliced
1 egg yolk mixed with a little milk

Cut the chicken into quarters. Heat a little butter in a large saucepan and fry the onion until golden. Add the chicken and brown well. Season with salt and pepper; add the wine and chicken stock. Tie the peppercorns, cloves and allspice in a small muslin bag and add to the pot. Cover and cook very gently for about 50 minutes until the meat is very tender.

Lift chicken from sauce, cool a little, then discard skin and bones. Break the meat into smallish pieces and set aside. Add the sago to the pot, cover and simmer for about 15 minutes until transparent. Remove from the stove, discard the spice bag and stir in the egg yolk to make a thickish, creamy sauce. Flavour with a little lemon juice. Mix chicken meat and diced ham into the sauce. Spoon half into a buttered pie dish. Arrange sliced hard-boiled egg on top and cover with the remaining filling. Cool to room temperature.

Set the oven at 200°C. Cover the pie with pastry, and decorate with pastry leaves. Brush with egg and milk and bake for about 20 minutes until the pastry is crisp and golden. Serve with Yellow Rice (page 71) and Blatjang (page 170).
SERVES 5

CAPE-MALAY CHICKEN CURRY

Malay curries have a glorious complexity of flavours and are usually more gently spiced than Indian curries.

1 large chicken, jointed,
or 1,5 kg chicken thighs
salt, milled black pepper
vegetable oil
2 large onions, roughly sliced
1-2 green chillies, finely sliced and seeded
2 sticks cassia or cinnamon
5 ml crushed garlic
5 ml crushed green ginger
15 ml Roasted Masala (page 217)
5 ml turmeric
5 ml ground cumin
5 ml ground coriander
2 ml ground cardamom
3-4 large, ripe tomatoes blanched, skinned
and chopped
500 ml warm coconut cream,
or Chicken Stock (page 216)

Remove and discard the chicken skin. Season meat with salt and pepper. Heat a little oil in a large saucepan and fry the onion until golden. Stir in the chilli, cassia or cinnamon, garlic, ginger, masala, turmeric, cumin, coriander and cardamom and sizzle for about 30 seconds (don't burn). Add the tomato and coconut cream or chicken stock.

Add the chicken to the pot, cover and simmer very gently for about 45-50 minutes until cooked. Check and adjust the flavour if necessary. Tip the curry into a warm dish, garnish with coriander leaves if you wish, and serve with rice, and sambals (see Chapter 13).
SERVES 4-6

CHICKEN BIRYANI

This famous Indian dish has its counterpart in the Cape Malay breyani or buriyani – often prepared for feasts by menfolk. There are numerous variations, including lamb, fish, prawn and vegetable, but chicken is the most popular.

1 large chicken, skinned and cut into pieces,
or 1,5 kg chicken thighs, skinned
salt, milled black pepper
2 ml saffron threads
250 ml warm water
375 ml white or basmati rice, rinsed
250 g brown lentils, rinsed
3 onions, sliced
Ghee (page 216), or butter and vegetable oil
6 potatoes, peeled and quartered
4 cinnamon sticks
6 cardamom pods, lightly crushed
6 hard-boiled eggs
fresh coriander leaves
MARINADE
250 ml buttermilk
60 ml chopped fresh coriander leaves
5 ml turmeric
2 ml ground cumin
2 ml ground coriander
10 ml Green Masala (page 217)
7 ml crushed green ginger
2 green chillies, sliced lengthwise

Season the chicken with salt and pepper and place in a non-metal dish. Combine the marinade ingredients, pour over and set aside for at least 3 hours.

Soak the saffron in the warm water for about 10 minutes. Parcook the rice in 1 litre salted boiling water for approximately 10 minutes. Drain well. Simmer the lentils in 500 ml unsalted water for 20 minutes. Drain well.

Fry the onions until golden in ghee, or butter and oil. Set aside. Fry the potatoes until golden. Set aside. Pour off most of the butter from the pan, add the cinnamon sticks and cardamom pods and sizzle for about 30 seconds. Stir in the rice; remove from the heat.

Set the oven at 160°C. Layer the ingredients in a large casserole: spread in one third of the rice, top with one third of the lentils, then the chicken with the marinade. Spread more rice on the chicken, then the onions and potatoes. Top with remaining lentils and rice. Pour the saffron water evenly over the surface. Seal with foil and cover with the lid. Bake for about 90 minutes until the chicken is cooked. Garnish with halved hard-boiled eggs and coriander leaves and serve with Dhal (page 165).
SERVES 6-8

POTROAST CHICKEN WITH DATES

Dates from the lush Orange River basin in the Upington area are delicious with potroasted chicken. It is important that the pot lid fits very well. If not, place a double layer of foil between pot and lid. It's a great recipe to do in a cast-iron potjie over the coals; once all the ingredients are added, there's no need to fuss with it.

1 large chicken
salt, milled black pepper
butter, vegetable oil
1 onion, finely chopped
1 stick cinnamon
6 whole cloves
5 ml turmeric
125 ml Chicken Stock (page 216)
125 ml medium-dry sherry
30 ml honey
15 ml lemon juice
15 ml Dijon mustard
2 ml crushed garlic
5 ml crushed green ginger, or 2 ml ground ginger
200 g pitted dates, fresh or dried
finely grated rind of 1 orange

Season the chicken with salt and pepper. Heat a little butter and oil in a saucepan and brown the bird well all over. Remove from the pot, stir in the onion and braise until glazed and golden. Add the cinnamon, cloves, turmeric, chicken stock, sherry, honey, lemon juice, mustard, garlic and ginger.

Place chicken on top. Cover and cook very gently for 30 minutes. Add the dates and orange rind and continue cooking until chicken is done – about 30 minutes more.

Transfer chicken and dates to a warm dish, check the flavour of the sauce and correct the consistency if necessary. Add a little water if it's too thick; reduce by boiling, uncovered, if it's too thin. Pour over the chicken and serve with rice and vegetables.

SERVES 4

MUSTARD-GLAZED GAMMON

Before sugar was farmed, honey was used to preserve hams. 'Cape ham' – enormously popular in the eighteenth century – referred to legs of pork pickled in brine for a month, then hung in the chimney for three weeks to smoke. Modern technology saves us this hassle, and succulent gammon remains a special treat – especially at Christmas.

1 leg of gammon
1 onion, quartered
2 carrots, quartered
3 bay leaves
15 ml ground allspice
5 ml black peppercorns
MUSTARD GLAZE
whole cloves
125 ml smooth apricot jam
15 ml Dijon mustard
5 ml dry English mustard
30 ml wholegrain mustard
30 ml orange juice

Weigh the gammon to calculate the cooking time, allowing 20 minutes per 500 g. Place in a large saucepan, cover with cold water. Add the onion, carrot, bay leaves, allspice and peppercorns, cover and simmer very gently until cooked.

Set the oven at 200°C. Remove gammon from the cooking water, place in a roaster and allow to cool. Trim fat to a layer of about 10 mm and score in a diamond pattern with a sharp knife. Stud with cloves. Mix together the jam, mustards and orange juice, and brush all over.

Bake, uncovered, for 20-30 minutes until the outer crust is nicely glazed. Baste occasionally with the pan-juices.
SERVES 10-12

111

RACK OF LAMB
WITH ROASTED VEGETABLES

This modern recipe reflects a Mediterranean influence
on a classic British roast.

2 ribs of lamb, 4-5 chops on each
olive oil, sea salt, milled black pepper
garlic cloves, fresh rosemary sprigs
vegetables for roasting (green and red peppers,
courgettes, beetroot, small leeks,
pattypans, mushrooms)

Set the oven at 200°C. Prepare vegetables for cooking. Cut through the backbone of the chops to make carving easier. Clean the long bone. Carefully cut off the skin, leaving just sufficient fat for self-basting. Place on a roaster. Rub meat liberally with olive oil and season with salt and pepper. Pack cloves of garlic and rosemary sprigs between each chop. Arrange the vegetables around the joint. Brush with olive oil and season with salt and pepper.

Roast meat for 10 minutes. Reduce oven temperature to 180°C and roast for about 30 minutes more; the meat should still be pink inside. Place lamb on a warm platter and arrange vegetables around.
SERVES 5-6

TOMATO BREDIE

Bredies were introduced by Eastern slaves,
and soon encompassed ingredients such as cabbage,
beetroot leaves, spinach and sorrel. The name, though,
emanates from Madagascar, an island with strong
trade links with India and Malaysia.
The secrets of a great bredie lie in balanced spicing and properly
'smooring' (smothering or browning) the meat and onion –
so easy when potroasting in cast-iron potjies over the coals.
Long, gentle cooking means the meat practically falls from the
bone to become one with the sauce. Use very little additional
liquid, as the flavour should come from the moisture in the
meat and vegetables. Bredie is even better prepared
a day or two ahead and reheated.

1,2 kg stewing mutton or lamb, trimmed and cut
into neat pieces
salt, milled black pepper
flour, vegetable oil
2 onions, sliced
3 cloves garlic, crushed
5 ml crushed green ginger
4 cardamom pods
2 ml coriander seeds
2 ml fennel seeds
15 ml chopped fresh thyme
15 ml chopped fresh marjoram
1-2 small green or red chillies, sliced and seeded
1 kg very ripe tomatoes, blanched, skinned
and chopped
5 ml brown sugar

Season the meat with pepper and dust with flour. Heat a little oil in a large saucepan and brown the meat well, a few pieces at a time. Return all the meat to the pot, add the onion, garlic and ginger and braise over high heat until the onion turns a rich golden brown.

Crush the cardamom, coriander and fennel seeds with a pestle and mortar and add to the pot with the thyme, marjoram, chilli, tomato and brown sugar. Season with salt. Cover and simmer very gently until the meat is very tender, stirring occasionally. If the bredie becomes too dry, add a little water or stock. If it's too moist, remove the lid towards the end of the cooking time. This may vary between 1-2 hours, depending on the cut of meat. Carefully skim off any extraneous fat.

Serve with plain rice and boiled potatoes, or add the potatoes to the bredie during the last 30 minutes or so.
SERVES 4-6

VARIATIONS Replace the tomatoes with the following:
PUMPKIN BREDIE 1 kg cubed pumpkin. To the spices add a cinnamon stick.
GREEN-BEAN BREDIE 300 g green beans, trimmed and cut at a slant. Add 1 ml grated nutmeg to the spices.
WATERBLOMMETJIEBREDIE 800 g waterblommetjies, trimmed and soaked in salted water, 1 green apple, peeled and grated, or 1 bunch of sorrel, chopped. Add a little grated nutmeg to the spices.

Lamb with Lavender (page 114), with Samp and Beans (page 68), and Beetroot with a Tangy Sauce (page 73).

DENNINGVLEIS

This recipe, brought from Java by the Malays and one of the courses served during a Batavian rijstafel, has its origins in the Javanese 'dendeng', a dish originally prepared with the meat of water buffalo, which was cured with salt and spices, dried in the sun and fried in coconut oil. Tamarind – the pasty dried fruit of an Indian tree – is the traditional flavouring. If you cannot find it, substitute a dash of wine vinegar or lemon juice.

1,5 kg stewing lamb, trimmed and cut into pieces
vegetable oil
4 onions, roughly chopped
5 ml crushed garlic
1 green chilli, finely sliced and seeded
5 ml grated nutmeg
2 ml ground allspice
6 whole cloves
2 bay leaves
salt, milled black pepper
250 ml hot water
50 g dried tamarind seed

Brown meat in hot oil in a large saucepan a few pieces at a time. Remove from the pot and set aside. Add the onion, garlic and chilli and fry gently until translucent. Return the meat to the pot with the nutmeg, allspice, cloves, bay leaves and a little salt and pepper. Pour in half the water, cover and simmer very gently until the lamb is tender – this may take 60-90 minutes depending on the cut used. Add more water from time to time if necessary.

Meanwhile soak the tamarind in the remaining hot water. About 30 minutes before the end of the cooking time, strain the tamarind, discard the seed and add the liquid to the pot. Serve with rice and atjar, or with stewed, dried fruit.
SERVES 6-8

LAMB WITH LAVENDER

Long ago Hottentots dwelt in the Karoo with fat-tailed sheep.
Later the 1820 British Settlers introduced merinos, hardy sheep
that fed on aromatic wild veld bushes and grew fat and tasty.
This recipe comes from the Karoo, where both lamb and lavender
are plentiful – although you are welcome to use rosemary instead
of lavender if you prefer. Olden-day lamb recipes were extremely
rich as they were potroasted in their own fat, or the fat of the tail.
Nowadays cooks take care to remove all excess fat before cooking,
and choose oil to brown the meat in. We prefer lamb cooked long
and slow, so that it falls from the bone – pink-tinged meat is
seldom found in boerekos or in Cape Malay cooking, where roast
lamb is simply called boudvleis (leg meat).

1 large leg of lamb (about 2 kg)
salt, milled black pepper
500 ml buttermilk
grated rind and juice of 1 small lemon
125 ml olive oil
peeled cloves from 1 head of garlic
60 ml finely chopped fresh lavender leaves
large bunch fresh lavender
30 ml cornflour
250 ml cream
60 ml medium sherry

Place the lamb in a roaster and season with salt and pepper.
Mix together the buttermilk, lemon rind and juice, olive oil,
garlic cloves and chopped lavender, and pour over. Set aside
at room temperature for 3-4 hours (or refrigerate overnight).

Set the oven at 200°C. Place the lavender leaves on top of
the meat, cover with foil and roast for 30 minutes. Reduce
the oven temperature to 160°C and roast for a further
1½ hours until an internal temperature of 65°C is reached on
a meat thermometer. Turn meat occasionally. Place meat in
a clean roaster. Increase the oven temperature to 220°C and
roast, uncovered, for about 20 minutes to brown.

Mix together the cornflour and cream and add to the pan
juices, mashing the garlic cloves and whisking until the
sauce is smooth and thickened (buttermilk separates while
the lamb roasts). Stir in the sherry.

SERVES 8

GIEMA CURRY

Curried mince – or very finely chopped beef or mutton –
is an Indian and Cape Malay favourite. There are many
ways of spicing it, so feel free to accentuate your own particular
favourites. If you wish, pad out the recipe with cubed potato.
Any masala of your choice may be used to heat things up
instead of, or as well as, the chilli.

1 kg minced beef
vegetable oil
2 onions, chopped
15 ml crushed garlic
15 ml crushed green ginger
2 sticks cassia
4 cardamom pods, lightly crushed
4 whole cloves
4-5 curry leaves
2 red or green chillies, sliced and seeded
10 ml ground coriander
10 ml ground cumin
7 ml turmeric
400 g can whole tomatoes, chopped (don't drain)
70 g can tomato paste
salt, milled black pepper
500 g peas
6 hard-boiled eggs

Fry the onion in hot oil in a large saucepan until golden.
Add the garlic and ginger, then the cassia, cardamom,
cloves, curry leaves, chilli, coriander, cumin and turmeric.
Sizzle for about 30 seconds, then add the mince. Stir over
high heat until the meat is sealed and changes colour.

Mix in the tomatoes and tomato paste, and season with
salt and pepper. Cover and simmer very gently, stirring
occasionally, for 45-60 minutes until the meat is very tender.
Add a little boiling water only if the curry becomes too dry.
Add the peas and heat through. Garnish with quartered
hard-boiled eggs and coriander leaves if you wish.

SALOMI Prepare Roti (page 203) and wrap them around a
spoonful of Giema Curry.
SERVES 8

ROGHAN JOSH

Indian dishes are individually and uniquely spiced, which gives diners the experience of layers of flavours unfolding in the eating. Recipes are usually passed down by example from mother to daughter, rather than by the written word. This north Indian dish is extremely popular on the menus of Indian restaurants.

1,5 kg lean, cubed lamb
Ghee (page 216), or butter and vegetable oil
1 onion, chopped
1-2 green or red chillies, sliced and seeded
6 cloves garlic, crushed
15 ml very finely chopped green ginger
30 ml desiccated coconut
50 g slivered almonds, roasted in a dry frying pan
4 cardamom pods, lightly crushed
2 ml ground turmeric
125 ml plain yoghurt
2 ripe tomatoes blanched, peeled and chopped
7 ml salt
5 ml Garam Masala (page 217)

SPICE MIXTURE
15 ml ground coriander
5 ml ground cumin seeds
5 ml poppy seeds
2 ml ground fennel
2 ml ground cardamom
2 ml milled black pepper
1 ml ground cloves
1 ml ground mace

Toast the spices in a non-stick frying pan until aromatic, tossing them about with a spatular. Set aside and cool.

Heat ghee, or butter and oil in a large saucepan and fry the onion until golden. Add the meat and stir until lightly browned. Add the chilli, garlic, ginger, coconut, almonds, cardamom, turmeric and spice mixture. Stir in the yoghurt, tomato and salt. Cover and simmer very gently until the meat is tender, stirring occasionally. The cooking time may vary from 1-1½ hours depending on the cut used. Sprinkle with garam masala and cook for 5 minutes more. Transfer the curry into a warm bowl and serve with rice.
SERVES 6

1 kg minced lamb or beef, or a mixture of the two
butter, vegetable oil
2 onions, chopped
2 ml crushed garlic
15 ml curry powder
5 ml ground turmeric
2 slices bread, crumbled
60 ml milk
finely grated rind and juice of ½ small lemon
1 egg
5 ml salt, milled black pepper
100 g dried apricots, chopped
1 Granny Smith apple peeled, cored and chopped
60 ml sultanas
50 g slivered almonds, roasted in a dry frying pan
6 lemon, orange or bay leaves
TOPPING
250 ml milk
2 eggs
2 ml salt

Set the oven at 160°C. Butter a large casserole. Heat butter and oil in a saucepan and fry the onion and garlic until translucent. Stir in the curry powder and turmeric, and cook briefly until fragrant. Remove the pot from the heat.

Mix in the minced meat. Mix together the crumbs, milk, lemon rind and juice, egg, salt, pepper, apricots, apple, sultanas and almonds and mix in. Pile into the casserole and level the top. Roll up the leaves and bury them at regular intervals. Seal with foil and bake for 1¼ hours. Increase the oven temperature to 200°C. Mix together the topping milk, eggs and salt, (you may require extra topping if you've used a very large casserole), pour over and bake uncovered for a further 15 minutes until cooked and lightly browned. Serve with Yellow Rice (page 71) and Blatjang (page 170).
SERVES 8

RIGHT *Frikkadelle (page 117) served with Herbed Tomato Sauce (page 218). For koolfrikkadelle (cabbage frikkadelle) – also known as 'oumens onder die kombers' – wrap the meatballs in blanched cabbage leaves and simmer in beef or mutton stew.*

BOBOTIE

This would be a hot contender for South Africa's national dish! The recipe was selected for an international recipe book published in 1951 by the United Nations Organisation. Bobotie is a Cape-Malay creation, and they spice it up even more with cumin, coriander and cloves. A similar dish was known in Europe in the middle ages after the Crusaders had brought turmeric from the East. When our first Dutch settlers arrived, Holland was largely influenced by Italian cooks, and a favourite dish was a hashed meat baked with curried sauce, spiked with red pepper and 'sweetened with blanched almonds'. There are many local variations, but the idea is that the mince should be tender and creamy in texture, which means long, slow cooking. Early cooks added a little tamarind water; lemon rind and juice is a more modern adaptation.

FRIKKADELLE

1 kg minced lamb or beef or mixture of the two
1 onion, very finely chopped
60 ml chopped fresh parsley
5 ml ground coriander
2 ml ground cloves
5 ml salt, milled black pepper
2 slices bread
125 ml milk
1 egg, lightly beaten

Mix together the minced meat, onion, parsley, coriander, cloves, salt and pepper in a bowl. (If you enjoy the flavour of garlic, add a few crushed cloves to the mixture.) Place the bread on a flat plate, pour the milk over, crumble and add to the mince with the beaten egg. Set aside in a cool spot (or the fridge) for at least 30 minutes for flavours to mingle.

Form into 16 balls. Fry in oil over medium heat for 12-15 minutes until cooked, turning occasionally. Make sure that they are cooked through, without burning. Drain and place in a hot dish. Serve with Herbed Tomato Sauce (page 218). SERVES 6-8

OX TONGUE AND MUSTARD SAUCE

1 pickled (corned) ox tongue
5 black peppercorns
2-3 bay leaves
2 carrots, sliced
1 onion, sliced
2 ribs celery, sliced
1 bunch of fresh herbs (parsley, thyme, rosemary)
MUSTARD SAUCE
1 onion, finely chopped
50 g butter
45 ml cake flour
600 ml warm milk
15 ml Dijon mustard
5 ml dry English mustard
15 ml wine vinegar
salt, milled black pepper

Place the tongue in a saucepan with the peppercorns, bay leaves, carrot, onion, celery and herbs. Add sufficient cold water to cover the meat. Cover and simmer for 3-4 hours until tender. Remove the skin while still hot.

SAUCE Fry the onion in butter in a medium saucepan until translucent. Remove from the heat and blend in the flour, milk, mustards and vinegar. Season with salt and pepper. Simmer briskly until the sauce thickens, stirring constantly.

Slice the tongue and arrange on a serving platter. Offer the sauce separately.

SERVES 6-8

STUFFED OX TONGUE IN PASTRY

Speciality of Onze Rust, an historical restaurant near Bloemfontein in the Free State, presented in the photograph with Venison Pie (page 125).

1 pickled (corned) ox tongue
400 g puff pastry
MUSHROOM AND ONION STUFFING
1 onion, finely chopped
50 g butter
100 g button mushrooms, chopped
30 ml chopped fresh parsley
salt, milled black pepper

Cook and prepare the tongue as described in the previous recipe. Cut a hole in the tongue for the stuffing. Chop the meat that has been removed and set aside.

STUFFING Fry the onion in the butter in a medium saucepan until translucent. Add the mushrooms and parsley, season with salt and pepper, and cook, uncovered, for about 1-2 minutes until the mushroom is tender. Mix in the chopped tongue and allow to cool.

Set the oven at 180°C. Stuff the tongue. Unroll pastry and wrap the tongue to make a neat parcel. Decorate with leaves cut from the left-over pastry. Bake for about 30 minutes until the pastry is golden and crisp and the tongue is hot. Serve, if you wish, with Mustard Sauce (see previous recipe).
SERVES 8

TRIPE AND TROTTERS

'Pens en pootjies' was introduced by French Huguenots, who had a special way with offal. Karoo cooks perpetuated the recipe, cooking it inside a sheep's stomach when cooking utensils were unavailable. Cape Malays serve it at merang, a ceremony that began over 300 years ago, when slaves would gather to learn to read and write, practise their religion of Islam, and enjoy dishes their masters did not eat – like tripe and trotters, sheep's head and tongue. Purists believe it is sacrilege to add curry to tripe and trotters, so you're welcome to leave it out of the recipe! Ox tripe is just as good as sheep tripe.

tripe of 1 sheep (about 750 g), well cleaned
4 sheep's trotters
60 ml grape or cider vinegar
3 onions, sliced
10 ml curry powder
5 ml coriander seeds
5 ml ground allspice
5 ml turmeric
2 bay leaves
2 ml grated nutmeg
salt, milled black pepper
20 small onions, peeled
20 new potatoes, peeled

Cut the tripe into squares. Cut the trotters into 3-4 pieces, and remove glands in the natural split in the hoof. Wash and drain well.

Place trotters and tripe in separate saucepans, add 30 ml vinegar to each and cold water to cover. Cover and simmer gently for 1 hour. Drain the tripe (retain the stock) and add to the trotters with the sliced onion and sufficient of the stock to cover generously. Stir in the curry powder, coriander, allspice, turmeric, bay leaves and nutmeg, and season with salt and pepper.

Cover and simmer for 3-4 hours until the sauce has thickened, the tripe is extremely tender, and the bones will easily slip out of the trotters. About 30 minutes before the end of the cooking time add the onions and potatoes. Check and adjust the flavour if necessary. Serve with rice.

SERVES 6

ROAST QUAIL WITH BERRY SAUCE

Quail are either farm-bred or hunted, in which case they tend to be tougher and should be hung for 24 hours before being plucked and cleaned for cooking. This dish emanates from the KwaZulu-Natal Midlands, where both quail and raspberries are plentiful. We photographed it at the Old Halliwell Country Inn near Currys Post.

12 quails
50 g butter
honey, salt, milled black pepper
850 ml Chicken Stock (page 216)
80 ml Van der Hum, or another citrus-based liqueur
100 g fresh raspberries

Set the oven at 200°C. Heat the butter in a frying pan and brown the quails all over. Set the pan aside; it will be used to make the sauce, once the quails are cooked.

Arrange the birds in a roasting pan and spoon the butter over and add a trickle of honey. Roast uncovered for about 20 minutes until tender, basting once or twice. Season lightly with salt and pepper and place on a warm plate. Meanwhile boil the stock in an uncovered saucepan until reduced by half.

Reheat the frying pan, add the liqueur and flame. Pour in the reduced stock, bring to the boil and season with salt and pepper. Just before serving, add the berries to the sauce and heat through. Serve quail and sauce separately.
SERVES 6

OSTRICH MEDALLIONS WITH PEPPERED PINEAPPLE AND RED WINE SAUCE

*Ostrich meat is relatively new to the South African table,
even though the birds have flocked wild on our plains for
as long as anyone can remember. This recipe from Hunters
Country House on the Garden Route highlights our predilection
for combining fruit and meat to good effect.
If ostrich is unavailable, use beef fillet.*

8 plump ostrich fillet medallions
salt, milled black pepper
8 slices fresh pineapple, skinned, core removed
coarsely crushed black pepper

butter, vegetable oil
250 ml dry red wine
250 ml Meat Stock (page 216)

Preheat oven griller. Season the ostrich with pepper. Coat
the pineapple with crushed pepper, place on a baking tray
and place under the oven griller to brown. Keep warm.

Fry the steaks in a mixture of sizzling oil and butter;
remove from the pan and keep warm. Add the wine and
meat stock to the pan and simmer, uncovered, until sauce is
slightly reduced. Whisk in a knob of butter and season with
salt and pepper.

Flood four plates with sauce, top with ostrich medallions
and garnish with pineapple and fresh herbs.
SERVES 4

POTROAST GUINEAFOWL

Gamebirds like guineafowl need long, slow, moist cooking as the meat is very lean and tends to be tough. If guineafowl aren't available, substitute two small chickens.

3 guineafowl with giblets (not the livers)
250 g rindless streaky bacon, chopped
butter, vegetable oil, salt, milled black pepper
1 large onion, finely chopped
10-12 peeled cloves garlic
large bunch of fresh herbs
(parsley, thyme, oregano)
375 ml dry red wine
500 ml Chicken Stock (page 216)

200 g mixed dried fruit
200 ml port
45 ml marula or cranberry jelly

Pluck, gut, trim and halve the guineafowl. Cook the bacon until fairly crisp in a little butter and oil in a large saucepan. Stir in the onion and garlic and cook until translucent.

Lightly brown the guineafowl and giblets in the pot. Add the herbs, wine and stock, and season lightly with salt and pepper. Cover and potroast very slowly for 2-2½ hours until the birds are tender. Add the dried fruit about 30 minutes before the end of cooking. Place meat and fruit on a warm plate. Defat the sauce. Add the port and marula or cranberry jelly. Pour the sauce over and around the birds.
SERVES 8

ROAST LOIN OF KUDU
WITH BACON AND PINEAPPLE

*This modern venison recipe comes from
Bushmans Kloof Private Game Reserve, near Clanwilliam.*

1,5 kg loin of kudu
125 ml dry red wine
125 ml wine vinegar
salt, milled black pepper
500 g rindless streaky bacon
vegetable oil
1 pineapple, skinned and sliced

Tie string around the loin at regular intervals to keep it in shape. Place in a roaster and pour over the wine and vinegar. Cover and set aside for 5 hours to marinate.

Set the oven at 180°C. Lift meat from marinade, season with salt and pepper and wrap neatly with bacon. Reserve the leftover bacon for presentation. Return meat to roaster, and cook, uncovered, for about 45 minutes (it should still be slightly pink inside).

Meanwhile fry the extra bacon in a little oil until crisp. Fry the pineapple in the same pan until golden. Place the meat on a warm platter and garnish with bacon, pineapple and a bunch of fresh rocket leaves.

SERVES 8

VENISON PIE

The filling for this traditional Cape-Dutch pie is
made with fynvleis ('fine meat'), usually prepared
with those parts of the buck that aren't suitable for roasting,
like the neck or shin.

1,5-2 kg venison meat (on the bone)
vegetable oil
1,5 litres water
1 large onion, quartered
2 carrots, cut into chunks
2 ribs celery, roughly chopped
15 ml black peppercorns
1 bunch of herbs, fresh or dried
(parsley, bay leaf, thyme)
FOR THE PIE
125 g rindless streaky bacon, chopped
2 onions, sliced
5 ml crushed garlic
300 g button mushrooms, halved or quartered
250 ml sultanas (optional)
60 ml chopped fresh herbs
(marjoram, thyme, parsley)
salt, milled black pepper
45 ml cake flour
500 ml venison stock (from simmering the meat)
45 ml Dijon mustard
125 ml cream
400 g puff pastry
1 egg yolk mixed with a little milk

Brown the meat lightly in a little oil in a large saucepan. Remove from the pot and set aside. Add the water, onion, carrots, celery, peppercorns and herbs, cover and bring to the boil. Add the meat, cover and simmer very gently for 3-4 hours until it is so tender it falls from the bone. Remove meat from the pot, allow to cool and cut it into small chunks or shred roughly with your fingers. Be sure to discard all fat and sinews. You should have about 1 kg meat.

Return the bones to the pot and boil briskly uncovered until reduced by half. Strain and reserve 500 ml; freeze remaining stock, for later use.

Heat a little oil in wide saucepan and lightly brown the bacon, onion and garlic. Mix in the mushrooms, sultanas and herbs, and season with salt and pepper. Blend in the flour, stock, mustard and meat. Cover and cook gently for about 5 minutes. Remove from the heat and stir in the cream. Pour into a large pie dish and allow to cool.

Set the oven at 180°C. Cover the pie with pastry and decorate with pastry leaves. Brush with egg yolk and milk, and bake for about 30 minutes until the pastry is cooked to crisp, golden perfection, and the filling is piping hot.
SERVES 8

HERB-CRUSTED VENISON WITH ROSEMARY

2-2,5 kg leg of venison
fresh rosemary sprigs
milled black pepper, olive oil
60 ml chopped fresh herbs
(thyme, rosemary, sage)
ROSEMARY SAUCE
150 g cold butter, cut into blocks
6-8 spring onions, trimmed
250 ml dry white wine
stock from roasting the venison

Set the oven at 200°C. Lay out a sheet of heavy foil large enough to wrap the venison in; scatter rosemary sprigs over.

Season the venison with pepper, rub with olive oil and roll in the chopped herbs. Heat a little olive oil in a frying pan and brown all over. Wrap in foil, sealing tightly. Place in a roaster and roast for 20 minutes. Reduce the oven temperature to 160°C and cook for 40-50 minutes more or until done to the desired degree. Unwrap the meat, place on a platter, tent with foil and keep warm. Reserve the meat juices.
ROSEMARY SAUCE Melt 30 g of the butter in a saucepan and lightly brown the spring onion. Add the white wine and a rosemary sprig. Bring to the boil and simmer until reduced by half, then add the meat stock and simmer for 10 minutes. Discard rosemary and gradually whisk in the remaining butter, piece by piece, over low heat.
SERVES 8.

CHAPTER ELEVEN
KWAZULU-NATAL

CANE FIELDS, PINEAPPLE PLANTATIONS, SARDINES AND SEASHORES

THE LUSH, SUB-TROPICAL Garden Province is a culinary rendezvous between east and west, its flavours inextricably linked with its forebears – black people who migrated from central Africa during the Iron Age, early British and Scottish settlers, Mauritian immigrants who planted bananas, mangoes, lychees and pawpaws, and Indians who introduced richly spiced cuisines of their homeland. Contradictions in culinary terms; gastronomic bliss for those interested in traditional foods of a wide variety of people.

KwaZulu-Natal has been inhabited for many thousands of years. Ancient tools have been unearthed as evidence of Stone Age hunting camps, and folk who grew crops, kept herds of livestock and lived in peace in the nurturing environment. More recent history records that, though already inhabited by a few San and the remnants of Zimbabwe's Karanga tribe – accomplished metalworkers – the area was settled early in the seventeenth century by the Nguni people who came south through Mozambique from the great lakes' region of central East Africa. They built beehive huts of branches domed with plaited grass, formed family groups and lived in relative harmony. In time these people laid the foundations of the Zulu nation.

Their crops flourished in fertile soil, livestock grew fat, profilic plains' game augmented their diet of amasi (curdled milk), maize meal, gourds, millet and sorghum. Sorghum also forms the base of traditional beer, a potent brew with wide-ranging social importance in ceremonies and feasts – even in settling disputes!

Bowls of spices at Durban's Victoria Street market, ready for mixing into fresh masalas.

Durban beachfront by night – a vista of twinkling lights.

Zulu food is simple and sustaining, and includes dishes such as beans cooked with samp, pumpkin with maize meal, beef stew with dumplings, jacket-baked sweet potato and madumbe (a nutritious brown root). Marginally more elaborate is baby pumpkin layered with chopped pumpkin stalks and madumbe leaves.

The bright lights of Durban contrast dramatically with rural KwaZulu-Natal. The city is many things to many people – a pleasure-seekers' holiday spot, an industrial force to be reckoned with, and home to a multi-faceted, multi-national population who take pride in preserving their traditional ways of living and eating.

It is also one of Africa's principal cargo ports. Durban's natural harbour was formed some 150 million years ago when cataclysmic subterranean forces sculpted Africa's coastline, while subsequent changes were imposed by the sea's natural ebb and flow. Portuguese navigators named the harbour *Rio de Natal* (River of the Nativity) or *Parva de Pescari* (the fisheries) because fish traps made from wattle-fencing woven with reeds were set in the shallows by the Lala and Luthuli people.

Protected in the north by a sandspit and in the south by the high, bushy ridge known to Europeans as The Bluff, and to Africans as *isiBubulungu* (the long, bulky thing), the harbour lured seafarers and pioneering European, Indian Ocean island and Asian settlers to visit – and to stay. The motley collection of people included pirates, slaves and slave traders, merchants, shipwrecked sailors and war refugees.

They marvelled at the rich abundance of wildlife. Waters teemed with fish, waterfowl and hippos were plentiful, trees were alive with chattering monkeys and chirping birds. Plains' game and big game proliferated, including elephant – their tusks an irresistible attraction for ivory traders.

Voortrekkers came to establish their own state far from British oppression at the Cape, coinciding with the arrival of scatterlings from Shaka's efforts to build his mighty Zulu nation. Battles for supremacy ensued. In 1843 Natal became a British territory – a move motivated more to establish interracial harmony than enthusiasm for economic potential, which was limited to coal deposits and the possibility of cotton production. This lead to more strife as Boer and Brit fought each other for possession of the land.

From the ashes of this complex history rose a community who remember their shared roots and acknowledge battles that had to be fought before a measure of stability could be found.

The province's mighty sugar-cane industry began inauspiciously. First there was a species of wild sugar cane Zulus called *mpha*. Then an experimental cargo of 'red cane' was brought from Mauritius and auctioned to local farmers. A Mauritian, Ephraim Rathbone – on his way to become overseer of Edmund Morewood's cotton estate – persuaded Morewood to plant a crop, thereby launching an industry that today sustains thousands of cane farmers and hundreds of thousands of workers, and produces sufficient of the sweet stuff to satisfy both local demands and a lucrative sugar-export market.

In 1860 Indians were brought here under contract to work in the cane fields, creating not only a vital labour force, but impacting on the culinary ethic of the province. They came from varying linguistic, geographic, class and religious backgrounds, each stream remaining true to its individual cooking traditions. Hindu implies vegetarianism; Muslim means a more varied diet that includes meat but forbids pork. The

TOP *Pineapples for sale at a wayside fruit stall.*
CENTRE *A Zulu man sips sorghum-based beer from a traditional beer pot.*
BOTTOM *Bougainvillea blooms frame sub-tropical farmlands near Umhlali.*

cuisine of southern India differs from the north, favouring coconut, and rice rather than wheat, and a greater abundance of chillies. The magic threads that embrace it all are the myriad spices which transform the most fundamental ingredients into something extraordinarily exotic.

In tiny gardens were sown precious seeds of vegetables and herbs brought from home. Key foods and spices were imported. Improvisation became the mother of invention, and Indian housewives drew on local influences such as European (especially in cakes and desserts), African (pap, beans and suchlike), and even Cape Malay (bobotie, bredies and sosaties), to form a South-Africanised version of Indian cuisine.

RIGHT *A display of fresh East Coast rock lobsters.*
BELOW *Fishermen head out to sea on a perfect Indian Ocean dawn.*

South of Durban the Agulhas current follows the continental shelf, compressing a counter-current flowing northwards. This results in the extraordinary June 'sardine run', when vast shoals come close to shore, and fish are cast onto beaches in glittering heaps. Spotter planes alert fishermen to the abundant harvest, and 'sardine fever' ensues, infecting all who come to partake of the feast.

In a jumble of crumpled hills and valleys north of Durban – a land previously known as Zululand or KwaZulu (home of the Zulu) – is an area of visual splendour, agricultural significance and historical importance.

Though the coastal belt is hot and humid, cool sea breezes carry gentle rains to the high-lying hills, nourishing

LEFT *The smoke from cooking fires adds atmosphere to peaceful rural scenes.*
BELOW *Game birds and their eggs in a Midlands' pantry window.*

luxuriant vegetation, cane fields and pineapple plantations, and swelling rivers on their journey to the sea. Savannah and grasslands are interspersed by dense bush and thick forests – perfect for wild game, now protected in a multitude of private game reserves and conservation areas.

This is the heart of Maputaland, an early traders' route so richly described in H Rider Haggard's evocative writings. From here one can explore vast and varied areas encompassing diverse ecosystems – from Kosi Bay in the north to the huge wetlands area of Lake St Lucia in the south; from the Lebombo mountains in the west, to the fishing paradise of the Indian Ocean in the east.

The Midlands, inland of Durban, is a world of tranquil hills and peaceful vales, a mere 200 kilometres wide, embraced in the west by the Drakensberg, which forms a natural barrier with Lesotho. Zulus know these mighty mountains as *Ukathlamba* (the barrier); Sothos call them *Dilomo tsa Natal* (the cliffs of Natal), while settlers nicknamed them 'the mountains of the dragon' from legendary monsters that lived in the peaks.

The San, who hunted antelope on the Drakensberg's grassy foothills in days gone by, crossed this vast range at what is known as the Sani Pass, leaving behind drawings in the sandstone overhangs of the sheltering cliffs as testimony of their existence.

Today cattle graze where once antelope roamed free; modern highways leading to historical guest houses have replaced dusty byways that once clattered with the sound of ox-wagon wheels.

A network of rivers and patchwork of lakes and dams form the heartland of the trout fishing industry. The brown trout descends from the spawn of a couple of barrels that survived the trip from Scotland to Natal in 1890. Prosperous hatcheries now provide fish to stock other farms for fly-fishing purposes, and retail outlets for general consumption. Game birds are very much part of the hunting (and eating) scene and menus in the area offer these delectable birds in interesting recipes, often combined with local fruits.

Alien brambles, introduced in the fodder brought in for horses during the Anglo-Boer war, proliferate along highways and byways, providing berries for snacking, for making into jams, and to be woven into indigenous recipes. Piccanins pluck these 'jiccijollers' (the spelling remains a mystery even

TOP *Shortens Country House at Umhlali was built in 1903 by Horace Hulett, son of sugar baron, Sir Liege Hulett. The farm, now a guest house of note, borders the first sugar mill in southern Africa.*
BOTTOM *A tangle of brambleberries in a Midlands country lane.*

to locals) and offer them to travellers. Wild mushrooms and asparagus also grow freely – spears the size of pencils blooming after the first rains of the season in August.

A gourmet's overview of KwaZulu-Natal is far removed from those who first arrived and partook of the province's fish and veldfood. Menus reflect the nuances of the cuisines of all the province's peoples – oriental spices, Indian Ocean island abundance and colonial conservatism.

CHAPTER TWELVE
BRAAIVLEIS & POTJIEKOS

NECESSITY, THE CANNY MOTHER of invention, guided early cooks and shaped their culinary skills. Forever on the move, they bagged food from the veld, or fished it from sea and shore, and cooked it by the wayside over the coals of a fire. South Africans are among the most enthusiastic outdoor cooks in the world, and braaied meats and seafood, 'pot food' and toekos (side dishes) – eaten alfresco, of course – are the nation's favourite way to go for a casual meal.

The name vleisbraai (or braaivleis) was coined at early Cape fairs and festivals, where special events were celebrated. Matters would often get out of hand as the gathered throng made merry, and the focal point of the food was a variety of braaied meats.

Braaivleis began with venison and wild birds; later lamb, cattle and pork were sizzling on the grid. All parts of the animal were enjoyed, including the offal – a special treat.

The art of potjiekos, the ultimate one-pot fare, developed in tandem with the open-grid braai. This forgiving cooking method is suitable for any quality meat, because a cast iron pot creates all-round heat. Only occasionally is the lid lifted and the food basted; the secret is to keep the pot closed so that the natural juices can create an intense sauce.

Seashores, of course, are perfect places to find fishy snacks and, backdropped by crashing waves, a gentle breeze and a few fisherman's tales, braaiing your catch, or freshly-gathered shellfish is an appealing option.

A pot of pap (maize-meal porridge) or boiled potatoes, makes a delicious side dish, as do vegetables such as potatoes, onions, mushrooms, butternut and corn, wrapped in

LEFT *The sun sets on a perfect African bushveld scene, as a fire burns down in readiness for a braai.*
ABOVE *Butterflied Lef of Lamb (page 143) with new potatoes.*

foil, and nestled in medium coals, or cut into chunks, brushed with olive oil or butter and charred on the grid.

Other countries have enthusiastically adopted gas and charcoal braais which they call barbecues; here the allure of glowing wood coals reigns supreme – and fuel is a hotly debated topic! Winelands' braaiers, for example, consider

their wingerdstokke (vine stumps) superior to the Free State's dried maize cobs; rhenosterbos of the bushveld vies in the flavour stakes with the Western Cape's rooikrantz. The most important thing, though, is to gather family and friends around the fire, and cook up a feast of delicious braaied goodies, just as they did in the 'good old days'.

▲ *Boerewors (page 137) served with Herbed Tomato Sauce (page 218) and Maize Meal and Spinach Patties (page 66).*
▲

BOEREWORS

The origin of spicy 'farmer's sausage' is attributed to early German settlers who knew all there was to know about sausage-making. As mincing machines only came onto the scene in the nineteenth century, meat was previously finely chopped. Making boerewors is an individualised and satisfying (though time-consuming) task, one you won't want to do on the day of the braai; for the best flavour and tenderness, wors should mature for a few days in the fridge before being cooked. It may be frozen for up to three months. Besides being braaied, boerewors may be dried, though in this case a thinner sausage is usually made.

2 kg well-matured beef from the forequarter
1 kg fatty pork (neck, shoulder or belly)
45 ml coriander seeds
5 ml whole cloves
30 ml salt
15 ml milled black pepper
2 ml grated nutmeg
10 ml ground allspice
10 ml brown sugar
125 ml dry red wine or grape vinegar
90 g thick natural sausage casings, soaked in water

Trim the beef and pork of all sinews. Cut into long, narrow strips about 3 cm in diameter, and freeze for about 30 minutes. Mince through a coarse mincer for a rough texture; finely if you prefer. Feed through the machine with very little assistance from the tamper. Finish by mincing a piece of bread to remove the last vestiges of meat.

Roast the coriander and cloves in a dry frying pan until aromatic. Grind with a pestle and mortar and sift to remove husks. Mix with remaining spices and sugar, and sprinkle over the mince. Lightly mix in with the red wine or vinegar.

Drain sausage casings, place one end over the filling horn and push on, leaving a 10-cm length hanging down. Tie a knot in this. Feed sausage mixture into the mincer a little at a time, while securing the casing with gentle pressure on the horn to control the unrolling of the casing as it is filled. Mould the sausage uniformly with your hand. Don't pack the casing too full, or the wors will burst while cooking, and try to avoid air bubbles forming.

Remove the filled sausage – still attached to the horn – from the machine. Push remaining boerewors mixture into the casing and tie a knot in the end.

Braai boerewors quickly over hot coals. The skin should be crisp and the middle still slightly pink. Serve immediately.
MAKES 3,5 KG

SOUTRIBBETJIES

Crusty-crisp 'salt ribs' may be prepared with lamb or pork. The recipe was devised before refrigeration, when meat was preserved in brine made with water, saltpetre, coarse salt and brown sugar. As wood for coals is scarce in the Karoo, cooks there prepare a unique speciality called kliprib (stone ribs), which are 'baked' to perfection between red-hot rocks.

1,5-2 kgs rib of lamb or pork
15 ml coriander seeds
60 ml coarse salt
10 ml brown sugar
2 ml saltpetre

Trim the meat of excess fat and saw through bones so that the portions may be more easily cut after cooking. Slash the fat to allow it to cook away.

Roast the coriander seeds in a dry frying pan until aromatic and lightly browned. Grind with a pestle and mortar and mix with the salt, brown sugar and saltpetre. Rub into the meat, then place on a roasting rack for several hours in a cool spot with good air circulation.

Before braaiing soak the ribbetjies for 30 minutes in cold water, to get rid of the excess seasoning. If you wish, parboil to reduce the braaiing time and make the meat more tender. (This saves time, though there is a loss of flavour.)

Make sure you have sufficient coals for about 1 hour's cooking. Start with the meat high above the coals, to sizzle very gently and brown only slightly. Bring the ribs nearer the coals as they die down. Cut the tender, crisp morsels into finger-sized portions and serve as snacks with lemon wedges for squeezing, which adds a nice tart flavour.
SERVES 4

BOEREWORS AND MANGO KEBABS WITH MANGO SALSA

12 chunks Boerewors (page 137)

4 ripe mangoes

lemon leaves, olive oil

MANGO SALSA

1 ripe mango, pipped, peeled and cubed

¼ English cucumber, sliced and seeded

1 small onion, sliced, blanched and drained

SALSA Mix the mango, cucumber and onion in a small bowl. Toss with a little olive oil. If you wish to add a garnish, toast sesame seeds in a dry frying pan and scatter on top. Cover and chill.

KEBABS Peel the mangoes and slice fruit from pips. Thread onto skewers with boerewors and lemon leaves. Brush liberally with olive oil. Braai over medium-hot coals for 6-7 minutes until crisp and cooked, turning occasionally. Serve the salsa separately.

SERVES 4

CHARRED LIVER AND BACON
WITH FRIED ONION

Rural folk roast calf's liver while meat is being portioned, and the appetizing aroma fills the air, encouraging workers to finish quickly! Offering liver with onion and bacon has British overtones – flavours and textures are delicious in tandem – though more often fried than braaied. Venison, pig or lamb livers may be used, but delicate calf's liver is the most tender.

1 kg calf liver
butter, vegetable oil
3-4 cloves garlic, finely chopped
salt, milled black pepper
3 onions, sliced
12 thick rashers rindless back bacon

Rinse the liver in cold water and pull off the membrane. If it doesn't come off easily, soak for a few minutes in cold water with a dash of vinegar. Cut into thickish slices of about 2-3 cm, and cut out the large veins. Place in a bowl, pour a little oil over, add the garlic and lots of milled pepper, and toss gently to mix. Cover and set aside.

Fry the onion in butter and oil until golden brown in a frying pan over the coals. Keep warm.

Heat a hinged grid until piping hot. Drain the liver (don't dry it), clamp in the grid and braai very quickly over hot coals for about 1-2 minutes on each side. The outside should be crisply charred; the inside tinged with pink. Meanwhile crisply sizzle the bacon on the grid. Arrange liver on a platter, season with salt and top with fried onion and bacon.
SERVES 6

Muise ('mice') are an old Cape delicacy, and are also known as vlermuise (bats) and skilpadjies (little tortoises). A similar favourite – chopped liver mixed with meat – is stuffed into the large intestine before braaiing. Some cooks prefer to mince or finely chop the liver and mix it with breadcrumbs, chopped onion and currants. A more modern method is to use larger chunks of liver.

MUISE

500 g lamb liver
1 lamb caul (netvet)
milled black pepper
15 ml coriander seeds
Worcestershire sauce, lemon wedges, sea salt

Rinse the liver in cold water and pull off the membrane. If it doesn't come off easily, soak for a few minutes in cold water with a dash of vinegar. Cut into finger-sized oblongs and season lightly with pepper. Spread the caul on a board and cut into pieces large enough to enfold pieces of liver. Wrap and secure with toothpicks.

An hour or two before braaiing, roast the coriander seeds until aromatic in a dry frying pan, and grind with a pestle and mortar. Scatter over the muise and sprinkle liberally with Worcestershire sauce.

Braai quickly on both sides over high heat - they should still be pink in the centre. Serve as they come off the grid with lemon wedges for squeezing, and a little sea salt.
SERVES 4-6

MASALA LAMB CHOPS

*Although braaiing meat over the coals is not
indicative of Cape-Malay cooking, this marinade reflects
their favourite flavours.*

6-12 lamb chump, loin or leg chops
(1-2 per person)
salt, milled black pepper
MASALA MARINADE
125 ml vegetable oil
60 ml chutney
30 ml lemon juice

15 ml crushed garlic
10 ml crushed green ginger
10 ml ground coriander
5 ml crushed red chillies

Trim the chops and season with salt and pepper. Stir together the marinade ingredients in a flat non-metal dish, add the chops and turn to coat. Cover and set aside for about 4 hours. Turn occasionally to flavour evenly.

Braai over medium-low heat for about 5 minutes until crisp on the surface and pink within. Serve with Braised Malay Rice with Peas (page 70) and Mealie Wheels (page 151).
SERVES 6

SOSATIES

Taverns in old Cape Town were known as Sosatie and Rice Houses in honour of these delicious kebabs. Like many spiced, semi-preserved dishes, sosaties were popular padkos (road-food) for ox-wagon and horse-drawn carriage journeys. Any type of meat will do, including beef, ostrich or pork. Bacon is acceptable, but finely textured fat slivers from around sheep's kidneys is best - it melts and moistens while cooking.

1 large leg of lamb (2-2,5 kg), boned and cubed
125 g dried apricots
sheep's fat or rindless streaky bacon
MARINADE
2 large onions, skinned and quartered
125 ml white grape vinegar
375 ml dry red wine
12 lemon leaves, bruised
3-4 thin slices green ginger
15 ml brown sugar
45 ml curry powder
30 ml ground coriander
5 ml ground allspice
2 ml ground cinnamon
2 ml ground cumin
10 ml salt, milled black pepper
1 ml ground cardamom

Place the lamb in a non-metal dish. Combine the marinade ingredients in a saucepan, cover and simmer for 5 minutes. Cool, then pour over the meat, turning to coat well. Cover and refrigerate for 3-5 days, turning meat once or twice a day.

Place the dried apricots in a small bowl, pour boiling water over, and leave to plump for an hour or two.

Cut the fat into the thinnest slivers possible, or bacon into squares. Thread with meat, apricots and onion (from marinade) onto skewers. Return the sosaties to the marinade until braai time. Cook over hot coals, basting with marinade, for 15-20 minutes. The lamb should still be pink in the centre.
MAKES ABOUT 16

Keema Seekh Kebabs served on Yellow Rice (page 71), accompanied by Sweet Carrot Pickle (page 167), Blatjang (page 170), Mango Atjar (page 169) and Pickled Vegetable Atjar (page 169).

KEEMA SEEKH KEBABS

Spiced minced meat on skewers is a famous Indian dish, one which is believed to have emanated from the royal cuisine adopted from Moghul emperors who invaded India in past centuries.

500 g minced lamb
5 ml Green Masala (page 217)
5 ml crushed garlic
5 ml crushed green ginger
2 ml ground cumin
2 ml ground coriander
5 ml salt
2 ml turmeric
30 ml chopped fresh coriander leaves
1 onion, grated or very finely chopped

Mix all the ingredients together. Form into balls and thread onto skewers, pressing firmly and packing them tightly together. Braai over hot coals for about 8 minutes, turning frequently so that they brown and cook evenly.
SERVES 8-10

BUTTERFLIED LEG OF LAMB

*Boneless meat is easier to carve, and cooks more
quickly over the coals. Braai in a domed braai
(barbecue), or cover the meat with a metal roaster to
trap and circulate the heat. Rosemary and lavender
are lamb's perfect herbs, especially if it is
South Africa's Karoo lamb, so much more
flavourful than any other. Toss herbs onto the coals
as well, for aromatic smoke.*

2 kg leg of lamb, or 1,5 kg boned lamb
salt, milled black pepper, vegetable oil
ORANGE AND ROSEMARY BASTE
125 ml olive oil
125 ml dry white wine
grated rind and juice of 1 orange
5 ml crushed garlic
30 ml chopped fresh rosemary or lavender
30 ml chopped fresh parsley

Boning a leg is easier if it is well chilled. A shortish, razor-sharp knife with a pointy tip and firm, narrow blade is essential. Start where the bones are visible, working with short movements, scraping meat from bones. Cut off the shank. Remove the pelvic bone, starting from the chump end. Remove the marrow bone: cut through the meat covering the bone, scrape away the meat surrounding the bone and pull it out.

Score the fat with a criss-cross pattern and season the meat with salt and pepper. Mix together the baste ingredients. Heat the grid and brush with oil. Lightly oil the lamb to prevent it from sticking. Brown over hot coals. Baste liberally, raise the grid, and cook over more moderate heat. Maintain the cooking speed by augmenting the coals, or by lowering the grid as the coals die down.

Turn and baste meat frequently as it cooks, which will take 50-60 minutes. An internal temperature of 70°C on a meat thermometer means medium meat – still rosy in the thicker parts. Cook a little longer if you prefer it well done.

Allow meat to rest in a warm spot for about 10 minutes before carving – across the grain – into thick slices.

SERVES 6-8

OXTAIL POTJIE IN RED WINE

*British settlers popularized oxtail in their
adopted country. It is essential that the cooking time is
long and slow, as the vegetables should cook away in
the gravy and the meat should be exceptionally tender.
Oxtail is even better prepared ahead and reheated.
When potjikos competitions were
all the rage in the 1970s, this dish was a
regular extrant!*

1,5 kg oxtail pieces
flour, vegetable oil
2 large onions, peeled and
finely chopped
2 large carrots, peeled and
finely chopped
2 ribs celery, finely chopped
1 large turnip, peeled and finely chopped
1 fresh or dried bunch of herbs
(bay leaf, thyme, oregano)
grated rind and juice of
1 small lemon
5-6 ripe tomatoes, blanched, skinned
and chopped,
or 400 g can whole tomatoes,
chopped (don't drain)
375 ml Meat Stock (page 216)
250 ml dry red wine
salt, milled black pepper
20 small onions, peeled

Dust the oxtail with flour. Heat a little oil in a large potjie and brown meat well in batches so as not to overcrowd the pan. Stir in the onion, carrot, celery, turnip, herbs and lemon rind and juice. Add the tomato, stock and wine. Season with salt and pepper, cover and simmer very slowly for about 2 ½ hours. Stir occasionally.

Add the onions, and continue cooking slowly until they're done and the meat is very tender. Skim off the fat and check and adjust the seasoning if necessary. Serve with rice or boiled potatoes.

SERVES 6

TANDOORI CHICKEN

Indian folk introduced exotic recipes like this one at a time when South African dishes were noted for their blandness.

1 small chicken
7 ml Green Masala (page 217)
5 ml crushed green ginger
5 ml crushed garlic
5 ml turmeric
250 ml buttermilk
1 pineapple, skinned and sliced

Cut the chicken through the backbone to hinge open. Place in a non-metal dish. Mix together the masala, ginger, garlic, turmeric and buttermilk, pour over and marinate in the fridge for at least 5 hours – overnight is even better. Remove chicken from marinade; pour marinade into a saucepan.

Braai chicken over medium-hot coals, turning occasionally until done. This should take 30-40 minutes depending on the heat. Do not baste while cooking, as the skin won't get nice and crisp. At the end of the cooking time roast the pineapple on the grid until lightly browned.

Place the chicken on a warm plate and garnish with pineapple. Warm the marinade and serve separately.

SERVES 2-3

BRAAIED FISH
WITH APRICOT GLAZE

Westcoasters have braaied their snoek this way for many, many years, and the firm, tasty flesh goes well with the tangy, fruity glaze. Any fresh linefish may be used. For added flavour, scatter fresh herbs on the coals as the fish cooks. If the weather is less than perfect, cook it under the oven griller.

1 whole fish, about 3 kg
salt, vegetable oil
125 ml smooth apricot jam
45 ml Worcestershire sauce

Behead the fish and cut into two fillets. Salt lightly and lay in a cool spot to air-dry for 1-2 hours. Rinse off excess salt.

Heavily oil the fish skin and flesh, and a hinged grid, and place the fish in it. Mix together the jam and Worcestershire sauce and liberally brush the fish's flesh. Do this while you wait for the coals to die down to allow the flavours to penetrate. Close the grid and braai fish, flesh down, over hot coals until beautifully browned. This will take approximately 5-10 minutes, depending on the heat of the coals. Turn the fish, baste again, and cook, skin down, for a further 2-3 minutes until cooked through. Serve with lemon wedges for squeezing.

SERVES 8-10

Braaied Fish with Apricot Glaze, prepared with yellowtail, and a roman being prepared for Salt Crust Fish (page 146).

SALT-CRUST FISH

Salt works extremely well as a sealing agent for whole, small fish.

4 fresh fish, gutted (scales, heads and tails on)
coarse salt, lemon wedges

Scatter a thick layer of salt in a dish large enough to accommodate the fish in one layer. Rinse fish and place – still dripping wet – onto the salt. Press firmly to coat well. Spread another layer of salt on top and press well into the fish. Set aside for several hours to flavour.

Lift fish carefully (retain as much salt as possible) and place gently on a well-oiled hinged grid. Braai over medium coals until done right through – 7-10 minutes on each side.

Place fish on a board and crack open the salt crust – skin and scales will lift off at the same time. Serve with lemon wedges for squeezing.
SERVES 4

A fresh trout ready to wrap in foil for Fish in Foil.

FISH IN FOIL

Foil is a substitute for natural wrappings like banana leaves. This is a cooking method best for delicate sea or freshwater fish weighing less than 2 kg.

4 fresh fish, scaled and gutted,
heads and tails on
butter, salt, milled black pepper,
lemon juice
2 ripe tomatoes, sliced
1 onion, finely sliced
fresh fennel fronds

Butter pieces of heavy foil large enough to wrap fish individually. Season fish inside and out with salt, pepper and a squeeze of lemon juice. Fill the cavities with tomato, onion and fennel. Top with a few pats of butter. Wrap securely and cook on the grid over medium coals; 7-15 minutes per side, depending on size and thickness of fish. Remove fish from foil and sizzle quickly over the coals for added flavour before serving, or serve directly from the foil parcel.
SERVES 4

FIGS IN BACON

During the short fig season, this is a favourite side dish at a braai. If you wish, prepare a day ahead; braai shortly before serving. Refrigerate, covered, until braai-time.

ripe, firm figs
rindless streaky bacon

Peel figs and wrap in rindless streaky bacon, securing the ends with toothpicks. Braai over hot coals until the bacon is crisp and the figs are hot.

COAL-ROASTED GARLIC

whole heads of garlic
olive oil

Tear squares of heavy foil, large enough to wrap the garlic in; allow two pieces for each. Remove excess 'paper' covering the garlic, break heads open slightly and place on the foil. Drizzle a little olive oil over, and enclose to make neat parcels. Nestle in medium-cool coals for 45-60 minutes until tender. Unwrap and pop out the perfectly-cooked garlic cloves to serve with meat or baked potatoes.

BRAAIED LOBSTER

*Braaiing is the time-honoured way of preparing lobster –
at the seaside between layers of freshly gathered seaweed,
or over the embers of a driftwood fire. Fresh (within a
day or two of catching) is best and – to connoisseurs –
the only way to eat it. Freezing takes its toll on
both flavour and texture.*

4 large, fresh lobsters, or lobster tails
salt, milled black pepper
Garlic and Herb Butter (page 217)

Place the lobster on a board, belly down, tail outstretched.
Rest a large, sharp knife down the length of the back from
the small horn between the eyes. Press down or hit the
knife with a mallet to split the shell neatly, then cut through
the tail. Scrape out and discard entrails, rinse and pat dry.

Season lobster with salt and pepper, brush with garlic
herb butter and place flesh down on a well-oiled grid over
medium coals. Cook just long enough to lightly brown the
meat. Turn, baste liberally and cook for a further 10-15 minutes until the flesh is opaque and pulls easily away from the
shell. Serve with Mayonnaise (page 218).
SERVES 4

LOBSTER WITH LEMON GRASS AND CORIANDER CREAM

Stalks of lemon grass create nifty handles for braaiing lobster tails. They also impart a delicious flavour which calls to mind an Oriental influence. The sauce is not obligatory, but it rounds off the dish splendidly.

8 large lobster tails
9 long stalks lemon grass
60 ml olive oil
10 ml sesame oil
5 ml crushed garlic
2 ml crushed green ginger
60 ml medium sherry
CORIANDER CREAM
½ bunch fresh coriander leaves, well washed, dried and finely chopped
finely grated rind of ½ orange
45 ml orange juice
125 ml sour cream or plain yoghurt
10 ml soy sauce
5 ml sesame oil
1 ml salt

CORIANDER CREAM Mix ingredients together. Chill.

Deshell and devein the lobster tails. Trim the ends of eight of the lemon grass fronds, remove the tough outer layers, and cut to suitable lengths. Impale lobsters with lemon grass, and place in a non-metal bowl.

Finely slice the remaining lemon grass and place in a small bowl. Whisk in the oils, garlic, ginger and sherry, pour over the lobsters and set aside to marinate for about 3 hours.

Braai over medium-hot coals for about 6 minutes until cooked and lightly browned. Serve with coriander cream.
SERVES 6-8

PERLEMOEN IN KELP

It must have been a very intuitive cook who first placed perlemoen (abalone) in the belly of a freshly-cut piece of sea bamboo and cooked it in the embers of a fire! Butter and grated nutmeg may be added, but the flavour is so profound, that it really is not necessary. A simpler way to braai perlemoen is to season the tenderised steaks with a little salt and pepper, dip in melted butter and braai on the grid over hot coals for about 2 minutes per side.

2 large perlemoen
2 large bulbs of kelp, each about
60 cm long

Remove fish from shell and scrub well to remove the greenish film (a pot scourer works well). Trim the frilly 'skirt' and dark area where the alimentary canal is situated. Cut the meat into thick slices. Tenderise lightly with a mallet then pack into the kelp. Plug the holes with clean cloths (do not use a stone as a stopper; the build-up of steam in the seaweed may cause it to shoot out).

Place kelp in the hot embers of the fire (there is no need to wait for coals to form) and cook for 20-30 minutes depending on the size of the chunk of seaweed. Turn once during the cooking time.

Slice off the top of the kelp and tip out perlemoen and sauce into a warm dish. Offer with crusty bread.
SERVES 4-6

COAL-ROASTED CORN

Fresh green mealies (also known as corn, sweetcorn and maize) are most often simply boiled and buttered, however they are delicious roasted over the coals. It is important that the mealies are fresh – straight from plant to fire if this is at all possible. Buy them husks and all, for the silk is a good indicator of quality. Kernels should be plump and shiny.

fresh green mealies or sweetcorn
salt, melted butter

Fold back the leaves, and strip mealies of their silk. Replace the leaves. Immerse in cold water for 30 minutes, then braai over hot coals for 20-30 minutes. Brush occasionally with melted butter until the kernels are smoky and delicious. Turn frequently to ensure even cooking.

Mealies may also be braaied without the soaking or wrapping procedure, when their kernels attain a wonderful

SEAFOOD POTJIE

*Coastal fishing communities love to cook
seafood in potjies, incorporating fish, shellfish and molluscs,
rather like a bouillabaisse of Marseilles.
Select ingredients as the whim takes you and, of course,
depending on the availability of seafood.
Any firm white fish or gamefish is suitable.*

1 kg filleted, skinless fish
4-5 lobster tails
400 g large headless prawns
400 g calamari tubes, well cleaned
36 black mussels, or 900 g can mussels,
drained
60 ml olive oil
2 onions, sliced
4 large, ripe tomatoes, blanched,
skinned and chopped,
or 400 g can whole tomatoes, chopped
(don't drain)
5 ml crushed garlic
5 ml turmeric
60 ml chopped fresh parsley, or 10 ml dried parsley
salt, milled black pepper

Cut the fish into large blocks. Devein the lobsters and prawns (leave shells on). Cut the lobsters into chunks. Slice the calamari into rings. Rinse the mussels with cold water; if using fresh mussels, pull out the beards.

Heat a large potjie over the coals, add the olive oil and lightly brown the onion. Stir in the tomato, garlic, turmeric and half the parsley, and season with salt and pepper. Add about 125 ml hot water. Cover and simmer for 5-6 minutes. (Scrape away some of the coals to maintain a gentle heat.)

Nestle the fish and lobster into the sauce, cover and simmer for 5-6 minutes. Immerse the calamari and mussels in the sauce (add a little more hot water if necessary). Cover and simmer very gently for 1-2 minutes until the mussels open, the calamari is opaque and the seafood is cooked. Check the seasoning, scatter remaining parsley over, and serve at once with crusty bread.
SERVES 8-10

toasty aroma and flavour. Brush occasionally with butter to keep them moist. Serve warm, sprinkled with a little salt and smeared with butter.

MEALIE WHEELS Slice the mealies through into rounds before braaiing – this reduces the cooking time – or slice through afterwards, which makes them easier to eat.

VENISON AND PRUNE POTJIE

*The meat of wild game constituted our earliest potjiekos,
although another olden-day favourite was porcupine, which
would be de-quilled and encased, skin and all, in wet clay or
flour-and-water dough, and cooked in a hole dug in the ground
below hot coals. After a couple of hours, the casing would be
cracked open and the skin came away with it leaving behind
perfectly cooked meat.*

2,5 kg leg of springbok or impala
20 dried prunes
250 ml muscadel
125 ml brandy
4-5 cloves garlic, cut into slivers
salt, milled black pepper, vegetable oil
250 g rindless streaky bacon, cut into chunks
1 onion, very finely chopped
2 carrots, very finely chopped
4 whole cloves
4 juniper berries
5 ml ground allspice
2 ml ground coriander
2 ml ground nutmeg
30 g (30 ml) soft butter
30 ml cake flour

Combine the prunes, muscadel and brandy in a small saucepan, cover and bring to the boil. Set aside to plump.

Stud the meat with slivers of garlic and season with salt and pepper. Heat a little oil in a large potjie, add the bacon and cook until all the fat has rendered.

Add the meat and brown all over. Stir in the onion and carrot, then add the cloves, juniper berries, allspice, coriander and nutmeg, and the liquid from the prunes. Cover and potroast the meat for about 1½-2 hours until tender. Turn the leg every 30 minutes or so. Add the prunes to the pot about 15 minutes before the end of the cooking time. Remove venison from the pot and keep warm.

Mix together the butter and flour to form a paste and whisk into the boiling sauce little by little until it thickens. Check flavour and consistency, and adjust if necessary.

SERVES 8-10

POTBROOD

*Our burgher forebears took bread dough (risen with
dried hops or fermented must - crushed raisins), shaped it into
balls and nestled them in the fragrant depths of bredies.
At other times they baked the dough in cast-iron pots set
in a coal-fired hole in the ground, or on a bed of coals
next to their campfires. Baking potbrood is the
ultimate test of a braaier's skill, for one needs to carefully
judge the heat of the coals to cook it without burning,
and purists reserve pots for this purpose alone.
Potbrood vies for top honours with pap (maize-meal porridge)
and potatoes as an accompaniment to braaied meat.
Any bread dough recipe may be used; this is a simple
white potbrood.*

1 litre cake flour
2 x 10 g sachets instant dried yeast
5 ml sugar
5 ml salt
30 ml vegetable oil
250 ml warm water (approximate amount)

Sift the flour into a large mixing bowl. Mix in the yeast, sugar and salt. Make a well in the centre and pour in the oil and water. Mix to a nice dough (depending on the absorbency of the flour, it may be necessary to add a little extra water), then knead for a few minutes until smooth and elastic. Place in an oiled bowl, cover lightly with oiled plastic wrap (this keeps out draughts and allows you to watch what's happening at the same time) and leave in a warm spot until double in bulk.

Punch down the dough, and place in a well-buttered small potjie. Cover as before and set aside in a warm spot to rise until double in bulk.

Place the potjie on a bed of cool coals (if your pot has legs, press them into the soil). Pile a spadeful of coals on the lid to crisp the crust as it cooks. The cooking time will vary according to the heat of the coals – about 1-1½ hours should be sufficient. When a metal skewer comes out clean and the loaf sounds hollow when tapped, the bread is cooked. Cool on a rack. Serve with butter.

MAKES 1 LOAF

Xhosa women in the eastern Cape prepare Potbrood and Samp and Beans (page 68) over their fire.

ROOSTERKOEK (Grid Bread) Prepare a fairly stiff dough (reduce the amount of liquid specified). If the dough is too wet, it will drip through the grid before the heat has time to crisp the outside! Shape bits of dough into small balls between floured palms and place on a clean grid over medium coals. As soon as the underside is crisp, turn carefully and cook until they sound hollow when tapped.

ASKOEK (Ash Bread) Bread rolls cooked directly in the coals of the fire have a charm all of their own. For extra flavour, use milk or buttermilk instead of water. Form into flattish cakes the size of your palm and place in the ashes of a cool fire.

As soon as they are charred and crusty, they are ready to eat. Split and serve hot with butter.

WINDMILLS AND WHEATFIELDS, SUNFLOWERS AND SHEEP

Two rivers form the boundaries of this gently undulating prairieland – the Orange in the south; the Vaal in the north. Inbetween are thousands of farms, a random scattering of rural towns and villages, and, to break the monotony of the horizon as you hurtle along the highway between the Cape and Gauteng, gently undulating oceans of maize and wheatfields, flocks of fat, contented sheep, and windmills standing stark against a brilliant sky.

In the eastern highlands savannah sweeps on to meet the mighty Drakensberg, or 'dragon mountains', where the boundaries of the Free State, KwaZulu-Natal and the kingdom of Lesotho, home of the Basotho, meet atop the Mont-aux-Sources. Five rivers rise in the aptly named 'mountain of beginnings', including those that embrace the Free State.

The myriad name-changes of this province echo the path of its human and political history. As evidence of his sojourn, sheltered by sandstone caves in the eastern hills, the long-vanished San left stone implements, bone arte-facts, and magnificent, mysterious rock art – the true meaning of which baffles experts to this day. By studying the ancient images of the most prolific of the world's prehistoric artists, we know that they hunted vast herds of plains' game like springbok, blesbok, hartebeest, gnu, zebra and quagga. Other clans like the Leghoja, Basotho, Barolong, Korana and Griqua followed the San to the hunting grounds.

The mighty Orange River was called !Garib (great river) by the Khoikhoi, for it was the greatest in the land; the area beyond was called Transgariep. In 1779 Colonel Robert

 Golden wheatfields in the summer sun are a common sight alongside the highway between the Cape and Gauteng.

The Artists' Colony, a tiny Free State guest house at Smithfield, built in the early Karoo architectural style.

Gordon, explorer and commandant of the Dutch East India Company, renamed it in honour of the Prince of Orange. The area beyond the river became Transorangia.

Early in the nineteenth century white hunters were lured to this sun-splashed, game-rich plateau. When word of the lush soil reached the Cape, trek-farmers, in the crippling grip of a prolonged drought in the settled southern farmlands, came in search of good grazing. The Voortrekkers followed the farmers, and the tussle for land ownership and name-changing continued. The governor of the Cape Colony later claimed the province for Britain, and named it the Orange River Sovereignty. In 1854 the Republic of the Orange Free State was proclaimed by the boers. During the Anglo-Boer War the name changed again – to the Orange River Colony. In 1910 it became the Orange Free State, one of the four provinces of the Union of South Africa. After the general elections in 1994, it was finally named Free State.

Though gold and uranium are mined here, the rich soil remains the Free State's most enduring claim to prosperity – tenuous as this can be in times of drought. Because wheat grows so well, it is known as the 'bread basket' of South Africa. Bread also spawned the naming of the town of Bethlehem in the sandstone foothills of the Maluti Mountains, for Christ's birthplace means 'house of bread.' The river running through the valley, and on which the town was founded, is named the Jordan.

The Free State also grows goodly amounts of groundnuts, sunflowers, potatoes, onions, peas, beans and pumpkins, and more asparagus than anywhere in the country. Wild asparagus was well known to early Cape colonists, who gathered the tender sprouts, nicknamed it cat briar, and included it on early menus. Old documents record that it grew well in Jan van Riebeeck's vegetable garden, and was enjoyed by passing seamen. Many years later, at a Roman

157

Catholic monastery in Harrismith at the foothills of the Platberg in the eastern Free State, a horticulturalist experimented with cultivating wild asparagus. Seeds were later imported from America. Full-scale farming commenced in the 1950s, and today fresh and canned asparagus is produced both for the home and export markets. The difference between white, green and purple asparagus is how and when the spears are picked. White asparagus is harvested before the tips push through the ground. The spears quickly turn green in sunlight and, if left for a day or so, become tinged with purple.

Pretty Ficksburg, on the banks of the Caledon River (which the Basotho people call the Mohokare, or 'willow trees' after the willows that line its banks), bordering Lesotho is the hub of the country's cherry industry, and celebrates by hosting an annual festival each November. Ripe, luscious berries and by-products such as cherry brandy and cherry liqueur, are enjoyed by cherry-lovers from far and near, and special cherry dishes are created by cooks at local restaurants and guest houses.

Bloemfontein, 'city of roses', judicial capital of the country and provincial capital of the Free State, started as a humble stock farm. The farmer's wife planted a flower garden beside a spring known as Mangaung (place of leopards). The spring was subsequently named Bloem Fonteyn (flower fountain) and the simple mud-brick farmhouse was remodelled into a grand residence, which was home to the first three presidents of the Republic of the Orange Free State.

Vrystaters have a reputation for generous, warm-hearted hospitality, which has a lot to do with the fact that most come from farming stock, for whom sharing a meal is an honour and a privilege. They care little for prissy cooking trends and changing food fashions, preferring hearty potfuls of the homely stuff that feeds body and soul in equal measure. This is something they identify with, and which they offer with pride to their guests.

It is similar on the restaurant front, and though the Free State may not be over-subscribed with upmarket establishments that echo those of Gauteng, the Cape or Durban,

Sunflowers, a happy signature of the Free State, are grown on farms producing seeds for sunflower oil.

ABOVE *Mealies and sweetcorn, a mutation of the earlier crop, are the foundation of the Free State economy.*
RIGHT *A pile of pumpkins ready for the market.*
OPPOSITE TOP *Isak and Dolf Bester at the Bainsvlei Farmers' Market on the outskirts of Bloemfontein.*
OPPOSITE CENTRE *Young cow herdsman at sunset.*
OPPOSITE BOTTOM *Farmers inoculate sheep on a farm.*

characterful guest houses and simple inns at wayside farms entice travellers to take time out at a slower pace, and to explore menus filled with time-honoured comfort food. Buffet tables groan under roasts, potjies and casseroles of curried tripe, bobotie and oxtail, tongue in mustard sauce, and pies of lamb, venison and chicken. Blesbok, indigenous to the region, liberally draped with bacon and slowly roasted to succulent perfection, often has pride of place.

Home cooks proudly recreate back-to-roots recipes passed down from mother to daughter – typical of the fare that city-dwellers are often too sophisticated to admit to enjoying, let alone cooking. Farmers, skilled in the art of sizzling chops, sausage, sosaties and ribbetjies over glowing embers of maize husks, have a true understanding of the pleasure of braaiing, and delight in the conviviality of communal cooking. Their wives prepare traditional salads and delicious home-grown, home-bottled chutneys, relishes and jams to accompany the feast, as well as to stock home-industry shops and trestle tables at fêtes and bazaars.

Small-scale farmers sell their cash crops at markets near larger cities, displaying their wares on the backs of trucks and bakkies, piled on picnic tables and arranged on brightly coloured canvas on the ground. Shoppers come for a bunch of carrots and bags of freshly-dug potatoes, or to stock up for a week on the freshest produce money can buy. On market day one may discover such traditional culinary delights as biltong, dröewors (dried sausage), tsammakonfyt (melon jam), biskuit (rusks), Hertzog koekies and farm

butter. Home-made sosaties and boerewors are roasted over open fires and wrapped in soft rolls; perfect food-to-go while you are shopping.

Life in the Free State is dominated by the changing seasons, which in turn influence the province's livelihood – large- and small-scale farming. The billowing white clouds and clear blue skies of spring give way to thunderclouds and darkening skies of summer. When rains have fallen and the sun breaks through, rainbows arch on the horizon. Autumn landscapes are tinged with warm russets and reds. Winter chills the central and southern flatlands and offers its own visual magic in the highlands and Lesotho – glorious snow-capped mountains only to melt again as the ancient cycle of the seasons begins once more.

CHAPTER FOURTEEN
SAMBALS
& PRESERVES

BEFORE INDIAN INDENTURED labourers arrived in KwaZulu-Natal, and Malay slaves were brought from the East, local dishes emulated the plain, solid fare of Holland and Germany. Interpreted through Asian eyes – for slaves became the cooks of early colonists, and the Indians brought with them a myriad spices – a bland and boring line-up indeed. An exciting patina of Oriental brilliance was quickly added to local menus, not least in the introduction of sambals, atjars, pickles and preserves.

Then, as now, cool sambals were served with hot dishes; hot atjars and chutneys with blander ones. Distinctive Indian raitas (with spiced yoghurt) and crunchy kachoomers (based on chopped or sliced onion), found favour too.

LEFT *Fresh fruit and vegetables ready for preserving and pickling, in a cool Karoo farmhouse kitchen.*
ABOVE *Pickled Kumquats (page 170).*

Fresh coriander and mint from the herb garden were the dominant herbs; chilli, cumin and dried coriander the favourite spices.

Atjar is a generic name for a variety of pickles. Some were, as they are now, imported; others freshly prepared or purchased from Indian and Malay markets and shops. Delectable chutneys made from an abundance of ingredients such as onions, tomatoes, apples, coconut and dates. Indian-style pickled mangoes, lemons, limes, dried fruit and vegetables provide additional tongue-tingling heat for those whose palates are turned on by fiery fare.

All these wonderful goodies were a revelation to 'Mittel Europa' folk more used to partaking only of potatoes, rice and overcooked vegetables with their meat. All find perfect expression when offered as an adjunct to a plain or spicy main dish, but particularly curries, bredies and suchlike.

In sweeter vein, fruit was turned into exquisite conserves and preserves, either served solo or – Malay-style – with afternoon tea or coffee. Drawing on their experience with tropical fruit, Malay cooks knew that, for the best preserves and jams, most fruits require only gentle steaming in their own juices, and impregnating with thin syrup. As far as possible, the intrinsic shape, texture and flavour of the main ingredient was retained.

Before the advent of modern supermarkets and time-strapped two-income families, pantries were lined with the wonderful home-made goodies found in this chapter.

But while the motivation to make chutneys, pickles and jams in the 'good old-fashioned way' may not be as strong nowadays as when we needed to capitalise on seasonal gluts of farm produce, and have on hand salad substitutes when fresh ingredients were hard to come by, many modern cooks know that preserving is a wonderfully therapeutic and rewarding way of whiling away quality time in the kitchen – not to mention a delicious way to delight both friends and family with the fruits of one's labour.

 Free State Quince Salad page (64), and Quince Preserve (page 171), presented at Onze Rust restaurant, Bloemfontein.

◆ Wash jars in hot, sudsy water. Rinse well and drain.

◆ Place jars open-side up on a baking tray, with lids alongside, and sterilize in the oven for about 20 minutes at 110°C. Bottles must be hot and dry when filled.

◆ Always use a large saucepan to prevent the mixture from boiling over. Only use stainless-steel saucepans.

◆ For sugar to dissolve more quickly in the mixture, warm in the oven before adding.

◆ Test setting point for jam by pouring a little onto a cold saucer. Give a gentle nudge – if it wrinkles, bottle it.

◆ Tilt jars to prevent air bubbles, and fill to the brim. If you are using metal tops, cover first with melted wax or waxed paper. Seal with the lid while still hot; label with contents and date.

◆ Store in a dry, cool, dark place for up to six months. Once opened – keep refrigerated.

QUINCE SAMBAL

Quinces were once so prolific that they were preserved by salting, drying and packing in wickerwork containers. They were also candied and, as in this Cape-Malay recipe, made into a sambal which is delicious with curry, as well as with smoked fish dishes. Unlike most sambals, which should be made shortly prior to serving, this may be made a day or two ahead.

1 ripe quince
salt
1 small onion, grated
2 ml crushed garlic
1 small red or green chilli, sliced, seeded
and finely chopped
30 ml sugar
30 ml lemon juice

Peel and core the quince, and grate coarsely or slice into the finest slivers. Pile in a bowl, sprinkle with salt and set aside for 1-2 hours. Rinse under cold running water, drain well, and dry thoroughly with a clean tea towel. Mix with the remaining ingredients, cover and chill until required.
MAKES ABOUT 250 ML

DHAL

Cape Malay dhal or dhai is wonderful with spicy breyanis.

500 ml thick, plain yoghurt
salt
5 ml crushed garlic
½ small green chilli, sliced, seeded
and very finely chopped
2 ml ground cumin
½ bunch fresh coriander leaves, well washed,
dried and finely chopped

Mix ingredients together in a bowl, cover and chill well.
MAKES 500 ML

BANANA SAMBAL

Bananas and plantains, grown here since the earliest times, are served fresh, baked, stewed and made into puddings and salads. If you wish this sambal to calm a fiery main course, omit the chilli.

3-4 ripe bananas
1 clove garlic, crushed
1 green chilli, sliced, seeded and very finely chopped
½ bunch fresh coriander leaves, well washed,
dried and finely chopped
15 ml lemon juice
250 ml thick, plain yoghurt
salt

Skin and slice the bananas. Mix together the garlic, chilli, coriander, lemon juice, yoghurt and salt. Gently stir in the sliced banana and chill for 1-2 hours before serving.

CUCUMBER SAMBAL Substitute banana with ½ English cucumber, coarsely grated and very well drained.

WALNUT AND CUCUMBER SAMBAL Substitute banana with 100 g chopped walnuts, 6 finely chopped spring onions, and ¼ English cucumber, grated and well drained.
SERVES 4-6

APPLE-MINT RELISH

This tangy Indian relish is quick to whip up and equally delicious with a curry or braaied lamb chops.

2 large Granny Smith apples,
peeled, cored and sliced
250 ml lightly packed fresh mint leaves,
washed and dried
10 ml cumin seeds
5 ml salt
2 ml crushed garlic
5 ml Green Masala (page 217)
15 ml lemon juice

Place all the ingredients in a food processor or liquidiser and blend to a thick purée. Tip into a bowl, cover and chill.
MAKES ABOUT 250 ML

DATE AND ONION SAMBAL

Dates play a vital role in Malay life. Vistors to Mecca bring them back home as gifts, and dates are one of the titbits offered to break the fast after sunset during Ramadan, which begins with the sighting of the new moon at the beginning of the ninth month of the Muslim calendar, and ends at the sighting of the new moon at the beginning of the tenth month.

1 onion, very finely sliced
salt
200 g fresh dates
1 green or red chilli, very finely sliced and seeded
125 ml cider or wine vinegar
10 ml brown sugar

Place the onion in a bowl and pour plenty of boiling water over it. Set aside for 5 minutes, then drain well. Salt lightly.

Stone and quarter the dates and toss in a small bowl with the onion and chilli. Mix together the vinegar and sugar in a cup until the sugar dissolves; pour over. Serve within a couple of hours of preparation.
SERVES 4

FRESH CORIANDER CHUTNEY

100 g (1 large bunch) fresh coriander (leaves and trimmed stems), well washed and dried
5 ml Green Masala (page 217)
2 cloves garlic
2 ml salt
2 ml ground cumin
30 ml lemon juice

Place all the ingredients in a food processor or liquidiser and blend to a thick purée. Tip into a bowl, cover and chill for up to 3 days.
MAKES ABOUT 250 ML

DRIED FRUIT PICKLE

250 g mixed dried fruit
125 ml brown sugar
7 ml chilli powder
5 ml ground cinnamon
5 ml dry English mustard
5 ml red mustard seeds
5 ml black peppercorns
5 ml turmeric
5 ml salt
1 ml ground cloves
125 ml malt or wine vinegar
125 ml vegetable oil
30 ml golden syrup
2 ml crushed garlic
1 ml crushed green ginger

Cut the fruit into fine strips or chunks (discard pips) and place in a bowl. Mix together the brown sugar, chilli powder, cinnamon, mustard powder and seeds, peppercorns, turmeric, salt and cloves. Add to the fruit and mix in.

In a small saucepan combine the vinegar, oil and golden syrup; heat gently until well mixed. Stir in the garlic and ginger, and mix into the fruit. Store in a clean jar, stirring occasionally. Refrigerate for 3-4 days before serving.
MAKES 500 ML

SWEET CARROT PICKLE

200 g carrots
30 ml golden syrup
60 ml brown sugar
2 cloves garlic, finely chopped
2 ml salt
1 ml turmeric
2 ml chilli powder,
or 1 red or green chilli, sliced and seeded
2 sticks cinnamon
80 ml vegetable oil

Peel the carrots and slice into slim sticks. Place in a serving dish. In a small saucepan combine the golden syrup, brown sugar, garlic, salt, turmeric, chilli and cinnamon. Stir over low heat until well blended and the sugar has dissolved. Remove from the heat and mix in the oil. Pour over the carrots and mix in. Set aside at room temperature for 1-2 hours. It may be refrigerated for up to a week.
SERVES 6

SWEET-SOUR PICKLED LEMONS

10-12 lemons (depending on size of
lemons and pickling jar)
500 ml sugar
80 ml coarse salt
15 ml turmeric
5 ml chilli powder
lemon leaves

Scrub the lemons lightly under running water and cut into quarters. Mix together the sugar, salt, turmeric and chilli in a bowl. Sprinkle a little into a large, sterilized pickling jar.

Pack in the lemon quarters and leaves, sprinkling each layer with more of the sugar mixture, until the jar is full. Seal and store in a cool, dark cupboard for a month before serving, turning the jar upside-down every day to ensure even pickling.

The lemon juice will have formed a brine with the spicy sugar, and the peel will be pickled.

167

BREAD AND BUTTER PICKLE

Bread and Butter Pickle served with Fish Sambal (page 40).

History sends us mixed messages about the origins of this pickle, and the advent of its strange name. Suffice it to say, it's delicious!

2 large English cucumbers (about 850 g)
300 ml water
60 ml coarse salt
3 onions, very finely sliced
1 large red or green pepper, finely sliced and seeded
250 ml sugar
250 ml white grape vinegar
5 ml red mustard seeds
5 ml celery seeds
1 ml turmeric
4 whole cloves

Slice the cucumbers very finely and place in a bowl. Heat the water, add the salt and stir until dissolved. Cool. Pour over the cucumber. Place a plate on top to weigh down. Place a plastic bag filled with ice blocks on top of the plate to keep cucumber nice and crisp. Chill in the fridge for 3 hours.

Tip cucumber into a colander and rinse well. Tip into a bowl and mix in the onion and red or green pepper.

Combine the sugar, vinegar, mustard seeds, celery seeds, turmeric and cloves in a medium saucepan and bring to the boil, stirring to dissolve the sugar. Pour over the vegetables. Fill hot, sterilised jars to the brim. Seal; store in the fridge.
MAKES ABOUT 1,2 LITRES

PICKLED VEGETABLE ATJAR

*Farmers' wives would incorporate 'all the babes and
sucklings of the vegetable kingdom' in their pickled vegetables,
for the younger they are, the better the result. Fruit and nuts
may also be added, including walnuts, blanched almonds,
sliced apricots and naartjie (tangerine) segments.
Allow colour, texture and availability to guide you
when making this recipe.*

750 g mixed vegetables (onion, cauliflower, broccoli,
red, yellow or green peppers, carrots, English
cucumber, green beans)
peeled cloves from 1 head garlic
PICKLING MIXTURE
500 ml wine or malt vinegar
200 ml water
30 ml brown sugar
5 thin slices green ginger
5 ml salt
5 ml black peppercorns
5 ml turmeric

Cut all the vegetables uniformly – in slices, batons or florets
– so they cook evenly. Combine ingredients for pickling
mixture in a large saucepan. Cover and bring to the boil.
Add prepared vegetables and simmer uncovered for about
4-5 minutes until tender but still slightly crisp.

Cool the atjar slightly, then fill hot, sterilized jars. Seal and
store in a cool, dark place. Atjar improves with age, but
should be kept refrigerated once opened.
MAKES ABOUT 1 LITRE

MANGO ATJAR

*This Javanese atjar recipe is one of the oldest recorded,
and each district in the homeland has its own version.
The earliest Cape-Malay green mango atjar differed
from this more modern Indian recipe in that the fruit was stoned,
sliced and soaked in water for several days,
then dried and dressed with garlic, fenugreek, turmeric,
chilli and curry powder cooked in oil.*

1 kg (5-6) green, unripe mangoes
1 onion, thickly sliced
100 g slivered almonds
5 ml salt
250 ml sugar
375 ml malt or wine vinegar
2 green or red chillies, sliced and seeded
30 ml crushed green ginger
15 ml crushed garlic

Peel and slice mango from pips, and cut each slice in half.
Place in a large saucepan with the onion and almonds.
Sprinkle with salt. Add remaining ingredients, stir gently to
mix, cover and simmer for 15 minutes.

Uncover and simmer fairly briskly for 10-15 minutes
more, until the sauce thickens sightly. Stir occasionally.
Bottle in a hot, sterilized jar and seal while still warm. Store
in a cool, dark cupboard. Refrigerate once the bottle has
been opened.
MAKES ABOUT 1 LITRE

CHILLI JAM

*This fiery 'jam' is fun to make, keeps for weeks in the
fridge and will perk up anything from a braaied chop
to a bowl of avocado soup!*

200 g large, fat red or green chillies
200 g onions, finely sliced
250 ml sugar
125 ml water
2 ml salt
30 ml lemon juice

Slice the chillies and discard seeds if you wish; this makes
the jam less hot. Place in a medium saucepan with the
onion, sugar, water, salt and lemon juice. Bring slowly to the
boil, stirring until the sugar dissolves.

Cook uncovered over high heat for about 10 minutes until
the sauce thickens. Allow to cool. Pack in hot, sterilised jars,
seal and store in the fridge.
SERVES 8

BLATJANG

*Before we learned to make our own chutney from ingredients
as diverse as apricots, dates, quinces and raisins, blatjang was
imported from Java, made from sun-dried prawns and shrimps,
which were pounded with a wooden pestle and mortar, and
shaped into masses resembling large cheeses.*
*Blatjang is the pride of Cape Malay-cuisine, and the recipe
is one of the oldest around. The name comes from one of the
constituents of the Javanese sambal blachang. Early food writer,
C Louis Leipoldt, described it as 'bitingly spicy, pungently
aromatic, moderately smooth and a very intimately mixed
association of ingredients.' There is nothing quite like blatjang to
add zest to curries or braaied meat. Adjust the amount of chilli
to suit your preference. Blatjang may be stored for up to a year,
but refrigerate once the bottle has been opened.*

250 g dried apricots, chopped
250 g seedless raisins
3 litres grape vinegar
4 large onions, finely chopped
4 cloves garlic, crushed
500 g brown sugar
200 g flaked almonds
30 ml salt
45 ml ground ginger
30 ml ground coriander
30 ml red mustard seeds
10 ml chilli powder

Combine the apricots, raisins and vinegar in a 5-litre
saucepan. Soak overnight to plump the fruit. Alternatively,
if time is tight, simply cover, bring to the boil and set aside
for about 2 hours.

Add the remaining ingredients, and cook uncovered over
medium heat, stirring occasionally at first, then constantly
towards the end of the cooking time, until the chutney has
reduced to about one-third, and is beautifully thick. It
should take 1½-2 hours. To know when it is ready for bottling, test the consistency by putting a little in the freezer to
cool. Pour into hot, sterilised jars, seal and store in a cool,
dark cupboard.

MAKES ABOUT 2,5 LITRES

PICKLED KUMQUATS

This pickle is best a month or more after preparation.

1 kg ripe kumquats
10 ml salt
750 ml sugar
375 ml wine or malt vinegar
20 black peppercorns
5 ml ground allspice
5 ml ground cinnamon
20 whole cloves

Wash, destalk and halve the kumquats, and remove pips.
Place in a saucepan with the salt and cold water to cover.
Cover and simmer for 20-30 minutes until tender. The
cooking time depends on whether the fruit was picked
underripe or whether it had ripened on the tree. Drain and
transfer kumquats to a clean pot.

While the fruit is simmering, combine the remaining
ingredients in a saucepan and bring slowly to the boil, stirring until the sugar dissolves. Cover and simmer for 10 minutes. Strain over the kumquats and simmer, uncovered, for
15-20 minutes until the syrup thickens slightly and the fruit
is tender. Stir occasionally. Bottle in hot, sterilised jars.
MAKES ABOUT 1 KG

CURRIED TOMATO CHUTNEY

2 kg ripe tomatoes, blanched, peeled and sliced
500 g onions, sliced
10 ml salt
10 ml curry powder
300 ml malt or wine vinegar
300 ml sugar

Place the tomatoes and onions in a large saucepan, cover
and simmer for about 20 minutes until soft. Add the remaining ingredients, stirring until the sugar dissolves. Cook gently, uncovered, for about 45 minutes until thickened. Bottle
while warm in hot, sterilized jars. Store in a cupboard.
MAKES ABOUT 1,5 LITRES

Pickled Vegetable Atjar (page 169) with Sweet-Sour Pickled Lemons (page 167), Blatjang (page 170), Sweet Carrot Pickle (page 167), Mango Atjar (page 169) and Dried Fruit Pickle (page 166).

QUINCE PRESERVE

Children once knew the delights of a ripe quince crushed on a rock with sea water and eaten with a little of the brine. Its high pectin content makes it ideal for jam, but quince may also be baked, added to bredies, or used in sambals and chutneys.

1 kg quinces (4 medium)
salted water
500 g sugar
1 litre water
2 ml crushed green ginger

Rub the fruit under cold running water to remove all the soft down. Peel, remove the seeds and slice the fruit. Soak in a bowl of salted water for about 30 minutes. Ensure that the fruit is submerged, otherwise it will discolour.

Place the sugar and water in a large saucepan and bring to the boil, stirring constantly until the sugar dissolves. Drain quinces. Add to the pot with the ginger, and simmer very gently, partially covered, until the fruit is soft and the syrup is richly coloured and thick enough to reach setting point. This will take about 1½-2 hours. Pack fruit in hot, sterilized jars and pour in the syrup. Seal and store in a cool cupboard.
MAKES 1 LITRE

ORANGE PRESERVE

Farmers' wives called their jams and preserves comfits, and stored them in a cool, dark pantries – in the past in earthenware jars with dried ox-bladders tied over the tops to seal them. Seville oranges make the best preserve, but as they have a very short season and are reasonably hard to come by, any orange may be used.

1 kg oranges

salt

1 kg sugar

1,5 litres water

45 ml lemon juice

Grate off the orange skin, leaving pith untouched (to enable the syrup to penetrate the fruit). Rub fruit with salt to prevent discolouration, place in a bowl and leave to stand for 30 minutes. Pour boiling water over, then set aside until the water is cold. Rinse oranges thoroughly, return to the bowl and add cold water to cover. Soak overnight to remove any bitter taste.

Cut a deep, narrow cross at the base of each orange and remove pips by rolling the fruit between your hands and squeezing gently. Place oranges in a bowl of boiling water until the outer layer is soft (about 20 minutes). Test by piercing with a match – it should penetrate easily. If you wish, the fruit may now be cut in half.

Combine the sugar, water and lemon juice in a large saucepan and bring slowly to the boil, stirring until the sugar dissolves. (Don't allow syrup to boil until the sugar has dissolved.) Add fruit and boil for about 60 minutes until translucent, and the syrup has thickened. Remove scum from the surface from time to time.

If syrup is ready before the fruit, add extra, thin syrup to the pot. If fruit is ready first, remove from the pot and boil syrup briskly until it thickens. In this case, return fruit to the pot and bring to the boil again before bottling.

Lift fruit from syrup with a slotted spoon and pack into hot, dry sterilized jars. If cut in half, place cut side against the jar. Fill to the brim with boiling syrup and allow to cool. Cover with waxed paper that has been dipped in brandy. Seal the jars.

MAKES 2 X 500 GRAM JARS

GREEN FIG PRESERVE

1 kg firm, ripe green figs (stems intact)

15 ml slaked lime

2,5 litres cold water

1,2 kg sugar

1 stick cinnamon

30 ml lemon juice

Cut a cross at the base of each fig. Mix the slaked lime in the water, add the figs and soak overnight. This ensures the fruit will be tender, yet have a crisp skin. Rinse thoroughly.

Place fresh water in a saucepan to immerse the figs, add fruit and boil for about 15 minutes until tender. Remove from the pot and drain in a colander. Make the water up to 2 litres. Pour back into the pot, add sugar, cinnamon and lemon juice, and bring to the boil, stirring until sugar dissolves.

Drop in the figs one by one and boil, uncovered, for about 45 minutes until translucent, and syrup has thickened slightly. Pack figs into hot, dry, sterilized jars; fill with syrup.

▲ MAKES 2 X 500 GRAM JARS

▲

GRAPE JAM

Early Dutch versions of korrelkonfyt – one of our most popular jams – included aniseed (5 ml tied in muslin and immersed in the simmering jam). Ginger and cinnamon reflect the influence of Eastern cooks. This jam is delicious with braaied or smoked fish.

1 kg green grapes, preferably seedless
500 g warm sugar
1 stick cinnamon
3 thin slices green ginger
30 ml lemon juice

Remove grapes from stalks. Remove pips (pull out gently using the closed end of a hairclip). Prick grapes several times with a pin and place in a large saucepan with cold water to cover. Cover, bring to the boil and cook for 1-2 minutes.

Add the sugar, cinnamon, ginger and lemon juice, and heat, stirring until the sugar dissolves. Boil uncovered until setting point is reached (30-40 minutes, depending on the size of your pot). Fill hot, sterilized bottles and seal.
MAKES ABOUT 600 ML

BOEREJONGENS

Kaapsche jongens (Cape boys) or boerejongens (farmboys) are great with cheese. The recipe is a legacy of the French Huguenots.

1,5 kg firm, ripe grapes (preferably hanepoot)
250 ml sugar
250 ml water
375 ml brandy

Cut grapes from bunches leaving short stalks attached. Prick berries several times with a needle. Warm sugar and water in a large saucepan, stirring until dissolved. Simmer, uncovered until the syrup thickens slightly. Remove from the heat and add the brandy.

Sterilize enough glass jars to accommodate all the grapes. While still warm, pack in the grapes and pour in the hot syrup. Store in a dark, cool place for several months.

A jar of Boerejongens with Vetkoek (page 207).

CHAPTER FIFTEEN
GAUTENG, MPUMALANGA & NORTHERN REGIONS

MARULA FRUIT, MOPANE WORMS, TROUT FARMS AND TEA

THE NORTHERN REGIONS ARE a treasure trove of inspired and unusual edibles – bliss for inquisitive gourmets, who will discover delicacies as diverse as marula fruit and mopane worms, as elusive as wild game and as prolific as subtropical fruit. Tea estates flourish, trout grow fat in crystal streams and limpid dams, wild mushrooms proliferate in lush forests, while nuts ripen in tranquil groves.

This physically diverse region stretches from the urban sprawl of Gauteng through misty hills and undulating vales of the Eastern Highlands to the splendour of Mpumalanga, past rugged escarpments and majestic mountains of the high-lying plateaux, to the sparse bushveld and savannahs of the Lowveld – big game country. Further north one discovers the Northern Province, home of the VhaVenda, where unravelling ancient culinary and social mysteries provides fascinating glimpses into past and future, old and new.

Johannesburg, city of gold, and Pretoria, jacaranda city, are springboards for exploring northern and eastern reaches. Though concrete jungles may not be as picturesque as coastal villages, or as alluring as country escapes, the variety of eateries more than compensates for the lack of charm. Restaurants cater for the full spectrum of pockets and preferences; haute cuisine rubs shoulders with homely fare, and every type of ethnic cuisine imaginable, while food-to-go stalls create business opportunities for informal-sector entrepreneurs on city streets and at sporting events.

Tranquil places and open spaces smooth the wrinkles of one's soul not far from Gauteng. Explore the majestic Magaliesberg and the North West Province. KwaNdebele (home of the Ndebele people), north-east of Pretoria, provides a fascinating glimpse of the history, culture, tradition and cuisine of this artistic tribe.

 Two lionesses and their cubs on a private reserve in the heart of Mpumalanga's 'big game' country.

Tea pickers of the Sapekoe Tea Estate near Tzaneen, taking their fragrant load to the factory.

Mpumalanga – unspoiled, unexploited and imbued with rural tranquility – is a world of gentle country pursuits. Yet these peaceful places once echoed with the clattering ox wagons of Voortrekkers, rang with sounds of battle during the Anglo-Boer war, witnessed the influx (and ultimate demise) of slave traders, pioneering gold-diggers, raiding bandits, fortune seekers and ivory hunters. Wild, wonderful, desperate times; gone, though not forgotten, and constantly brought back to life in the tales of those early days, told and retold, around crackling bush fires, and in the timeless relics left to remind us.

Tourists take quality time out at luxurious guest houses and enjoy cuisine as fine as one will find in the more culinary erudite regions of the world. Wayside tearooms, pubs and restaurants proudly prepare local produce, for near at hand is a profusion of gourmet ingredients. Wild mushrooms grow in pine forests and oak groves. Small factories dry them, and export an abundance overseas. It takes about twelve kilograms of fresh ceps to make one kilogram of the dried delicacy, and even though they are the favourite food of porcupines – ignorant as they are of the value of their favourite snack – they are still prolific.

Trout have been farmed in Mpumalanga since the mid 1950s, and farmers are at pains to produce fish of the correct size, with flesh of near-perfect texture and colour. Flesh texture relates directly to the condition of the fish which, interestingly, relates in part to stress levels!

Processing smoked trout is a hands-on affair. Fish are 'brined' in salt and water for a couple of hours. Larger fillets are cold-smoked; smaller fish are hot-smoked – a combination of cooking and smoking. Travellers through this pretty

GAUTENG, MPUMALANGA & NORTHERN REGIONS

part of the country are assured of trout feasts aplenty, prepared by cooks constantly dreaming up new ways of serving this tasty and versatile fish – trout salads and omelettes, creamy bisques, piquant pâtés and crusty-domed pies, not to mention whole trout with a variety of inventive fillings. Or, stop at a farm shop, and buy it fresh to take home.

Nelspruit is the centre of a vast citrus-growing region. Together with nearby White River, it also grows pecan and macadamia nuts, and subtropical fruit such as lychees, bananas, mangoes and avocados.

Bustling Tzaneen boasts large-scale tea estates that have sister farms in the Northern Province and KwaZulu-Natal, where the industry started in 1850. Rolling hills are shrouded with manicured tea bushes. Pluckers nip off the topmost leaves, toss them deftly into baskets, then carry their fragrant load to the factory for processing. There leaves are 'withered' in troughs of warm air, minced through rollers, fermented (oxidised), dried, cleaned and graded.

Due to widespread malaria, game-rich eastern areas were largely uninhabited until the late 1800s, though settlement burgeoned after the disease had been controlled. Animal tracks soon became Voortrekker wagon trails, then rough, tortuous coach routes used by transport riders carrying supplies from the coast to the eastern Transvaal goldfields, and to early farming settlements even further afield.

Where men went, their guns were soon to follow, especially to this treasure-land of wildlife. Hunters killed for both pleasure and profit, learning only later – once untold damage had been done – that culling, or killing for the pot, are the only conscionable forms of hunting.

Inspired by statesman Paul Kruger, spearheaded by conservationists, and implemented by the Transvaal Volksraad, the killing of elephants was curtailed in 1850; hunters were forbidden to shoot more game than they could consume, and pit-traps and snares were outlawed. Closed season was then declared to allow game to breed.

ABOVE *Panoramic view over the Westfalia farmlands and avocado orchards near Duiwelskloof.*
RIGHT *Delicious, just-cooked food-to-go on offer at a sporting event in Gauteng.*

Wildlife sanctuaries like the Kruger National Park were created in the rich savannahlands that sweep down from the great lakes of central Africa, across Zimbabwe, through Mpumalanga to Swaziland and KwaZulu-Natal. These areas sport the largest concentration of game reserves on the continent. As a result, the game population is increasing, and our most fragile assets – wild animals – are being properly cared for, creating a legacy for future generations.

The Northern Province, bordering Zimbabwe, is a mysterious place of quiet, unspoilt beauty, steeped in traditions rooted in the mists of time. In contrast to modern cuisine

179

Factory workers preparing smoked trout for packing at
Milly's Trout Farm near Dullstroom.

experienced in Mpumalanga and Gauteng, the land that
was previously known as Venda offers simple foods
enhanced by fascinating folklore. The VhaVenda people –
one of Africa's oldest tribes – have called this region home
since the early eighteenth century. Steeped in superstition,
the area whispers legends of forebears who followed the
beat of the domba drum across the mighty Limpopo in
search of sanctuary.

Not far from the neon-bright capital city, Thohoyandou,
there are sacred places – Lake Fundudzi and the Thathe
Vondo Forest, burial place of chiefs, where one may not
visit without permission from the current chief.

In clustered villages life goes on much the way it has done
for countless years. But, like the passage of many ancient
civilisations, modern life is making insidious inroads, and
time-honoured traditions are falling into disuse. Soon they
will fade from man's memory, leaving the community
poorer for its loss. Nowadays women seldom grind their
own maize meal for mukonde (King's porridge), but still
patiently stir it over open cooking fires, ladling layers onto
wooden plates to be peeled off and eaten one by one.

Soil in the south is rich, and yields maize, coffee and tea, as well as vegetables and subtropical fruit sold at raggle-taggle roadside markets. These are diet staples supplemented, on special occasions, with the meat of chicken, beef and goat.

Hot, arid northern parts of the province sustain little save sparse mopane-scrub, home to mopane worms. Chewy and pleasantly flavoured, they are roasted over open fires, or dried and reconstituted by 'frying' in salted water. Sadly, this delicacy is becoming scarcer. Some blame escalating farming in the low-lying places mopane worms love best; other claim the supply has been stripped to its present low levels by human consumption. Nowadays women travel as far afield as Botswana for worms.

Mighty baobabs, one of the largest trees in the world, which live for about one thousand years, dominate the landscape with their sheer bulk (stems average seven metres in diameter). They seem to have been planted upside-down; branches resembling roots reaching to the sky, while deep underground is another tangle which could be the original branches. Baobabs are useful trees: fibrous wood is macerated into rope and paper, pollen is used as glue, leaves are cooked and served as a vegetable. Pleasantly acidic seeds tingle the tongue, and are ground and roasted to make 'coffee'. Fruit is pounded into flour, mixed with milk and prepared as porridge. Fruit pods contain tartaric acid, which is why the tree is sometimes called the cream of tartar tree.

There are marula trees aplenty here, and marula fruit holds a special place in the scheme of things. In February and March ripe, golden fruit falls to earth and starts fermenting – and impromptu parties happen under every tree. Marula fruit finds its way into meat stews and vegetable dishes, and makes delicious beer – clear, sparkling and slightly aromatic. Superstition guides the hand of the brewer: fruit is cut with a knife fashioned either of wood or the bone of goats, sheep or antelope. A little of the brew is invariably set aside as an offering to appease the spirits. More appealing to Western palates is marula jelly, a perfect adjunct to venison dishes, which are a speciality in these northern regions of South Africa.

When next the lure of the open road beckons, head north along untravelled paths, explore places where a sense of calm still reigns, and enjoy to the fullest food grown in the rich soil of a bountiful region.

TOP *Trout hanging on racks ready for smoking. The rainbow trout is best suited for cultivation, as it is not averse to living in the crowded conditions prevalent in many of the breeding dams.*
BOTTOM *At Hazyview's informal farmers' market, piles of dried beans, pecan and macadamia nuts are sold.*

181

CHAPTER SIXTEEN
SWEETMEATS
& PUDDINGS

THERE HAS NEVER BEEN a shortage of ingredients to satisfy our passion for sweet things – we simply scoured the veld for fruit like kei-apples, quinces, wild medlars, sour plums and wild oranges.

We ate it ripe and bursting with flavour, seasoned it with salt, ginger, cinnamon and pepper, made fruit salads flavoured with nutmeg, cinnamon, rose water, lemon juice and naartjie (tangerine) peel – and invariably added a dash of wine, brandy or rum. For sweet treats during long journeys, Eastern-style mebos was prepared from sun-dried, salted apricots, and *plat perskes* (flat peaches) from mashed peaches, dried and rolled or folded.

Two types of wild fig grow in coastal sand dunes – Hottentot figs, which have large yellow flowers and juicy fruit, and sour figs which make delicious jam. In the Northern Province you will find marula (which also makes a heady liqueur) and baobab fruit – large, spongy and floury, with a pleasant, acidic taste.

When Indians came to work on KwaZulu-Natal cane fields they added mangoes, pawpaws, and loquats to our fruit bowls, and turned it into tangy chutneys and pickles to accompany their spicy dishes.

Two alien fruits were introduced during the Anglo-Boer war that began in 1899 and ended in 1902; brambleberries sprung from seeds brought from England in fodder for cavalry horses, and ran wild in the KwaZulu-Natal Midlands, while in the Northern Cape soldiers munched on dates from their ration packs from home, and pressed the stones into river banks, where they grew into majestic date palms.

LEFT *Strawberry fields in the Cape Boland, where shoppers are welcome to pick as much as they want to and pay according to weight. Scarecrows keep watch and frighten off berry-loving birds.*
ABOVE *Strawberry Mousse (page 187), served in antique cut-glass cups.*

The concentrated juice of fruit such as cherries, grapes and plums sweetened early desserts. Wild honey was gathered from hives in soft baobab trunks – a treat regarded by native epicures as the finest honey in Africa. The Garden Route's Outeniqua mountains are named for the Hottentot 'a man laden with honey' referring to bee-keeping which was recorded in the area as long ago as 1782.

The wide variety of milk puddings in our repertoire reflect our Dutch and Anglo-Saxon roots, though many recipes have acquired Eastern nuances, thanks to Cape-Malay cooks who adapted recipes in their own style, and added alluring spicings to please their own palates.

Interestingly, a shortage of milk in their Javanese homeland encouraged them to use coconut milk as a substitute. As a result, it was introduced to a variety of Cape dishes.

Visitors to our shores will find a host of international desserts with fancy sauces and extravagant garnishes, fine imported and local cheeses, and elegant dessert wines grown and made in the Cape winelands.

For a true taste of Africa though, take a closer look; enjoy the simplicity of sun-ripened fruit, and puddings that hark back to country kitchens and family dinner tables – unique recipes that pay homage to a land and people whose sweetest pleasures are the simplest ones.

184

FRIED DATES WITH ALMONDS

Date palms dot the landscape near Upington in the Northern Cape and an avenue of palms over a thousand metres long – one of the longest in the southern hemisphere – has been declared a National Monument. These Indian sweetmeats are fun to make when fresh dates are available.

400 g fresh dates
20 blanched almonds
Ghee (page 216), or butter

Slice into the dates, remove the seeds and press almonds into the hollows. Fry in sizzling ghee or butter until brown and crunchy. Drain on kitchen paper and serve cool.
MAKES 20

ALMOND KOLWADJIB

This is an adaptation of a softish, uncooked Malay sweetmeat traditionally made with Java rice. The name is derived from the Malayan or Javanese gula-wajek, and some old recipes call them kowadjik, colvagied and koevagiep. Add a dash of rose water to the mixture if you wish, and decorate with glacé cherries for extra colour.

100 g nibbed or ground almonds
125 ml desiccated coconut
250 ml rice
750 ml milk
2 ml salt
peel of 1 naartjie (tangerine)
5 ml ground cardamom
50 g butter
125 ml brown sugar

Toast the almonds and coconut in a dry frying pan until golden and aromatic. Set aside to cool.

Combine the rice, milk, salt, naartjie peel and cardamom in a saucepan, cover and simmer very gently until all the moisture has been absorbed and the rice is very soft – it should be almost mushy. Stir occasionally. Remove from the heat, discard nartjie peel and mix in the butter, sugar, almonds and coconut. Press evenly into a dish and chill. Cut into squares before serving.
MAKES ABOUT 42

TAMELETJIES

*Sweetmeats aptly named 'stick-jaw' were wrapped
in buttered paper 'kadoesies' (packets) and sold by Cape-Malay
vendors in the streets of Cape Town. Children
would gather dennepitte (pine kernels) in pine forests,
just as the offspring of the French Huguenots did when their
parents introduced the recipe to the Cape in the late 1600s.
It quickly became a favourite sweet treat amongst old and young
alike. Grated orange or naartjie peel may be
added instead of (or as well as) the nuts. Cape Malays
substituted pine kernels with soaked dried peas,
and called them ertjie-tameletjies. Another variation
called for butter nuts (seeds of an indigenous melon)
and bits of date.*

100 g pine kernels
or slivered almonds
500 g sugar
125 ml water
30 g (30 ml) butter

Toast the nuts in a dry frying pan until golden and aromatic. Tip onto a baking tray to cool.

Combine the sugar and water in a medium saucepan and stir over low heat until the sugar dissolves. (Ensure it does not boil before this happens.)

Boil uncovered, tipping the pot to and fro occasionally, until the syrup thickens and turns from clear to light golden. Remove immediately from the heat and stir in the nuts and butter.

Pour onto an ungreased baking tray and allow to cool and harden. Crack into pieces and store in a wax-paper-lined sealed container.

CHIKKI The Indian community substitutes pine kernels or slivered almonds with 200 g finely chopped mixed nuts (pistachios, almonds, cashews and peanuts), mixed with 50 g seedless raisins.
MAKES ABOUT 24 PIECES

FRIED PAWPAW

*Tropical KwaZulu-Natal is pawpaw country,
where the fruit was first cultivated in the 1800s
after an influx of Mauritian people had arrived.
This delicious pudding is a favourite among Indians,
so good at devising recipes that are
feather-light and mysteriously sweet.
Batter and fruit may be prepared a couple
of hours ahead; fry the pawpaw just before
serving, as it tastes best straight from the pan.
Banana is equally delicious in this recipe.
Peel and cut into chunks before dipping
into batter and frying.*

1 sweet, ripe pawpaw
(about 1 kg)
salt, ground cardamom
Cinnamon Sugar (page 219)
vanilla ice-cream
BATTER
200 ml cake flour
1 ml salt
15 ml castor sugar
150 ml milk
15 ml melted butter
2 egg whites

BATTER Sift together the flour, salt and castor sugar. Whisk together the milk and melted butter, and mix into the dry ingredients to form a smooth batter. The consistency should be like thick cream; add a little extra milk if necessary. Beat the egg white stiffly and fold in.

Slice the pawpaw in half lengthwise and scoop out and discard pips. Cut off the skin. Slice fruit vertically, into slices about 20-mm thick. Season very lightly with salt and a little cardamom.

Just before serving, dip pawpaw into batter and deep fry a few pieces at a time in hot oil until crisp and golden.

Drain well on kitchen paper. Serve warm with cinnamon sugar and a scoop of ice-cream. Alternatively, offer softly whipped cream or thin custard, warm or cool.
SERVES 6-8

STRAWBERRY MOUSSE

The famous Cape Town flower-sellers,
whose happy blooms once brightened most of Adderley Street,
were preceded by strawberry-sellers.
Besides making delicious desserts, strawberry leaves were boiled
to help create the whitest smiles – they removed tartar from teeth!
Gelatine was unknown until early in the twentieth century;
before that isinglass and seaweed were used
to set cold puddings.

500 g strawberries, washed and hulled
125 ml castor sugar
200 ml plain yoghurt
60 ml port or sweet sherry
30 ml (20 g) gelatine
250 ml cream

Purée the strawberries in a food processor with the castor sugar. Add the yoghurt.

Gently warm the port or sherry (don't let it boil), sprinkle the gelatine on the surface and allow to sponge. Stir in thoroughly. Allow to cool. Whizz into the strawberry mixture.

Whip the cream stiffly and fold in gently with a large spoon. Pour into glasses and refrigerate to set. Garnish, if you wish, with extra whipped cream piped on top, whole berries and thyme sprigs.

SERVES 8

MIXED BERRIES
WITH INDIAN CHEESE

*The good old days weren't the greatest time for berries – they
were only found in the KwaZulu-Natal Midlands growing
on brambles introduced in fodder brought from Britain to feed
the horses during the Anglo-Boer war!
Now berries are produced in the Cape Boland, as the soil and
sunny climate perfectly emulate areas in southern Europe
where berries grow best. Partnering these berries is a traditional
Indian dessert – seekhund or sikhund – which may be
served on its own if you wish.*

500 g mixed berries (strawberries,
Cape gooseberries, tayberries, blueberries)
INDIAN CHEESE
50 g nibbed almonds
250 g cream cheese or cottage cheese
125 ml castor sugar
2 ml grated nutmeg
5 ml ground cardamom
250 ml cream

Wash and hull the berries and pile into glasses or serving
bowls. Cover and chill in the fridge.

INDIAN CHEESE Toast the almonds in a dry frying pan.
Cool. Beat together the cream cheese or cottage cheese, castor sugar, nutmeg and cardamom until well blended. Whip
the cream stiffly and fold in with the almonds.

Pile the berries into tall glasses and top with generous
spoonfuls of Indian cheese.

SERVES 4-6

PORT WINE JELLY

*Birthday celebrations in the Cape colony always ended
with tart wine jelly served in tall jelly glasses and
accompanied by thin custard and home-made preserves.
Tschin-Tschou – seaweed jelly made by Hout Bay fishermen –
was made from lacy pink seaweed, and latterly from
dried seaweed. The charm of it is that no matter how much
seaweed is used, it doesn't get leathery – just firm like
Turkish delight! It also easily absorbs flavourings
such as sugar and lemon or vanilla essence, rose water and
crushed cardamom, and food colouring brightens it up.*

500 ml water
30 ml (20 g) gelatine
80 ml sugar
2 whole cloves
2 sticks cinnamon
250 ml port
15 ml lemon juice

Measure 125 ml of the water into a cup, sprinkle the gelatine on top and set aside to sponge. Bring remaining water
to the boil with the sugar, cloves and cinnamon. Stir until
the sugar dissolves – don't allow it to boil. Cover and set
aside for 15 minutes for flavours to infuse.

Stir in the gelatine until well dissolved, then add the port
and lemon juice. Strain into a bowl and chill for a couple of
hours in the fridge until set.

Break up the jelly and spoon into jelly glasses or small
dessert bowls. Serve with custard, if you wish.

SERVES 6-8

BAKED APPLES
WITH CARAMELISED PEARS

6 Granny Smith apples

36 whole cloves

45 ml medium sherry

80 ml brown sugar

100 g butter, cut into blocks

CARAMELISED PEARS

125 ml orange juice

4 pears, peeled, cored and sliced

1 stick cinnamon

60 ml runny honey

60 ml brown sugar

15 ml finely grated orange rind

Set the oven at 160°C. Butter a small, deep baking dish. Core the apples (leave whole) and score skin by cutting round the middles. Make six small incisions in each and insert cloves in the holes.

Stand apples side by side in the baking dish. Pour the sherry over, and sprinkle brown sugar on top. Pop about 5 ml butter in each and bake, uncovered, for 60 minutes, basting occasionally with the syrup.

PEARS Heat the orange juice in a frying pan, add the pears, cinnamon, honey, sugar and orange rind, and dot with the remaining butter. Cook briskly, uncovered, until the pears are soft and the sauce has thickened to a light glaze.

Place the warm apples on a serving plate, spoon the pears around and serve with custard or whipped cream.

SERVES 6

PEARS IN SPICED RED WINE

A menu speciality at Cape Town's Leinster Hall restaurant.

4-6 pears
200 g (250 ml) sugar
200 ml water
2 cinnamon sticks
3 whole cloves
finely grated rind of 1 orange
500 ml red wine

Peel the pears (leave cores intact). Choose a saucepan large enough to fit them snugly. Pour in the sugar and water, and add the cinnamon, cloves and orange rind. Bring to the boil, stirring until the sugar has dissolved. Reserve 80 ml of the red wine (to add later) and add the rest to the pot. Add the pears, cover and simmer for about 15 minutes until tender.

Transfer pears with a slotted spoon to a glass bowl. Boil poaching liquid, uncovered, until it thickens to a light syrup. Add the remaining red wine. Pour syrup over pears and allow to cool. Chill for up to 5 days.

SERVES 4

CINNAMON SUGAR PANCAKES

Early Cape Malay, Cape Dutch and Indian cookbooks all include recipes for pancakes. A charming eastern way to serve them (noted by both Cape-Malay and Indian food writers) is to layer them in a stack with whipped cream, toasted slivered almonds and chocolate vermicelli – specks of edible silver leaf too, for very special events. Early Cape colonists cooked them in special long-handed irons in the fire, and laced the mixture with Van der Hum or brandy.

250 ml cake flour
2 ml baking powder
2 ml salt
2 eggs
650 ml milk
30 ml melted butter or vegetable oil
15 ml brandy or Van der Hum
Cinnamon Sugar (page 219)

Sift together the flour, baking powder and salt. Beat the eggs and milk until foamy, then gradually beat in the flour. Stir in the melted butter or oil, and brandy or Van der Hum.

Heat a little oil in a small frying pan. Pour in a thin layer of batter, tilting the pan to distribute evenly. Fry on one side only for about 1 minute until lightly browned, then turn the pancake out onto a plate. Keep warm while making the remaining pancakes. Roll up and serve with cinnamon sugar and lemon wedges for squeezing.
SERVES 6

PUMPKIN FRITTERS

Generations of South Africans have enjoyed these soft fritters, especially the Cape Malays, who call them bollas, and serve them after sunset during their fast. They are delicious served as an accompaniment to curry or bobotie.

500 g skinned, pipless pumpkin, cut into cubes
1 egg, lightly beaten
180 ml cake flour
5 ml baking powder
1 ml cinnamon
1 ml ground mace
Cinnamon Sugar (page 219)
SYRUP
125 ml brown sugar
125 ml water
5 ml cornflour

Cook the pumpkin in a little salted water in a covered saucepan. Drain well. Mash with the egg, flour, baking powder, cinnamon and mace.

Heat a little vegetable oil in a frying pan, drop in spoonfuls of the batter and fry until golden on both sides. Alternatively fry in deep oil; they will puff up even more. Drain well on kitchen paper. Pile into a bowl.
SYRUP Combine the ingredients in a small saucepan and bring to the boil slowly, stirring constantly until the sugar dissolves. Boil briskly until syrupy. Serve separately, with cinnamon sugar to sprinkle on top.
MAKES 10-12; 5-6 SERVINGS

Hull berries and rinse lightly with cold water. Put in a saucepan with the castor sugar, cinnamon, lemon juice and water. Heat gently until the sugar dissolves and the juices run. Drain and discard cinnamon. Reserve the syrup.

Line a 1-litre pudding basin with bread, cutting the slices neatly to fit (a circle for the base, wedges for the sides). Spoon in the fruit. Cut more bread to fit the top of the pudding and press down. Pour the syrup over, then cover the basin with plastic wrap and place a saucer on top weighed down with something heavy. Refrigerate overnight.

Turn the pudding out onto a plate, pour any remaining syrup over, and garnish with mint sprigs and fresh berries.
SERVES 6

KHULFI

Ice-cream is the perfect way to end a spicy meal, and it is no wonder that this is a favourite on menus of Indian restaurants. Early recipes require milk to be condensed by slowly simmering in a pot. A can makes the task so much easier. This is a firm ice-cream; remove from the freezer a little while before serving.

500 ml full-cream milk
60 ml cornflour
100 g nibbed almonds
50 g pistachios, shelled and finely chopped
1 ml ground cardamom
397 g can condensed milk
15 ml vanilla essence or rose water

Measure 125 ml of the milk into a jug and mix in the cornflour. Toast the nuts in a dry frying pan. Cool.

Bring the remaining milk to the boil in a medium saucepan with the cardamom. Add the cornflour mixture and boil for 3-4 minutes, stirring constantly, until thickened. Remove from the heat and stir in the condensed milk, nuts and vanilla essence or rose water.

Pour into a metal bowl and place in the freezer. Mix well every 30 minutes or so. After a few hours it will be too stiff for stirring, so re-whip in a food processor or with an electric beater, until smooth and creamy. Re-freeze and repeat the whipping process a couple more times. Freeze.
MAKES 2 LITRES. SERVES 8-10

SUMMER PUDDING

The romantic notion is that this dessert was invented in Britain as a celebration of summer, when gardens are filled with ripening berries. In the early days of the Cape colony it was made with mulberries, and an early foodwriter suggested only fallen fruit – undoubtedly the sweetest – should be used. It must be made a day ahead, by which stage the bread has soaked up the fruit juice and the pudding has set nice and firm. Any soft berries may be used, including raspberries, tayberries, stoned cherries, blackberries, mulberries and strawberries.

1 kg ripe mixed berries
125 ml castor sugar
1 stick cinnamon
15 ml lemon juice
60 ml water
10-12 slices day-old white bread, crusts removed

SOUSKLUITJIES

Cape Dutch sweet dumplings (also called melk kluitjies and melk frummeltjies) were often included in wedding menus – this recipe, for 'Ouma van Wyk's Wedding Day Souskluitjies', is dated 1912! They were photographed at Onze Rust near Bloemfontein, Free State.

500 ml cake flour
60 ml castor sugar
15 ml baking powder
1 ml salt
5 ml ground cinnamon
50 g butter, cut into small cubes
3 eggs
200 ml milk
5 ml vanilla essence
melted butter
Cinnamon Sugar (page 219)

Sift the flour, castor sugar, baking powder, salt and cinnamon into a bowl. Rub in the butter until crumbly. Mix together the eggs, milk and vanilla essence, and mix in to make a thick batter.

Half fill a saucepan with water and bring to the boil. Drop in tablespoonfuls of batter, allowing space inbetween. Cover and simmer briskly for 6-7 minutes. Don't lift the lid while cooking, otherwise the souskluitjies will be flat.

Drain with a slotted spoon and place in warm serving bowls. Continue until all the batter has been used up.

Pour a little melted butter over the souskluitjies, sprinkle cinnamon sugar on top and serve warm.

SERVES 6

CARROT HALWA

This famous Indian pudding may be served warm or cool, plain or garnished with whipped cream and silver dragees.

500 g carrots
100 g slivered almonds
100 g butter
500 ml full-cream milk
200 ml sugar
5 ml ground cardamom

Peel and coarsely grate the carrots. Toast the almonds in a dry frying pan. Cool.

Melt the butter in a large saucepan, add carrots and fry over high heat for about 10 minutes until soft and lightly glazed. Stir in the milk, sugar and cardamom and simmer very gently, uncovered, for about 10 minutes more until thick and creamy, and the carrots are very soft. Stir occasionally; constantly towards the end. Remove from the heat and stir in the almonds. Serve, topped with cream, in small bowls.
SERVES 8-10

BUTTERMILK PUDDING

South Africa's light, luscious answer to France's crème caramel and Britain's baked custard, borrows a little from each of these classic desserts. After the first Cape dairy was established in the mid 1600s, buttermilk became enormously popular, and was offered to workmen and sick sailors. Traditionalists offer this pudding with honey and cream; a fruity sauce better balances the sweetness. Please remember that this is a very delicate custard, so choose a wide baking dish rather than a deep one to bake in, and ensure that the water in the bain marie comes as far as possible up the sides of the baking dish.

50 g soft butter
200 ml castor sugar
4 eggs, separated
500 ml buttermilk
15 ml vanilla essence
60 ml cake flour
1 ml salt
250 ml cream
ground cinnamon

Set the oven at 160°C. Lightly butter a wide baking dish. Cream together the butter and sugar. Mix in the egg yolks, buttermilk and vanilla essence. Sift in the flour and salt and fold in gently.

Whip the cream until it holds soft peaks. Whip egg whites separately until stiff but not dry. Mix cream thoroughly into buttermilk base, then fold in the egg white. Pour into the baking dish and sprinkle lightly with cinnamon. Place in a larger baking dish, add boiling water to come halfway up the sides, and bake, uncovered, for 1 hour until a metal skewer comes out clean. Serve warm.
SERVES 6-8

Queen of Sheba Cake (page 215), and Blancmange were introduced by British and French settlers. Flavourings included peach or buchu leaves, almond essence, grated lemon rind or whole cardamom seeds. The recipes were re-created at L'Institut Culinaire in Stellenbosch in the Cape winelands.

BLANCMANGE
WITH BERRY COULIS

750 ml full-cream milk
60 ml sugar
125 ml cornflour
1 egg, lightly beaten
15 ml vanilla essence
Berry Coulis (page 219)

Bring 500 ml of the milk to the boil in a saucepan with the sugar. Mix cornflour into remaining milk, stir in and simmer gently for about 3 minutes until thick. Stir constantly.

Remove from the heat and stir in the egg and vanilla essence. Pour into a lightly oiled mould or small heart-shaped moulds lined with muslin. Chill for 3-4 hours to set.

Turn out onto plate (or plates), pour the coulis around, and garnish with a profusion of fresh berries and mint.
SERVES 8

QUEEN'S PUDDING

British settlers were fond of puddings made with bread, and this – also called Queen Victoria Pudding – is a typical example.

150 g fresh white breadcrumbs
45 ml castor sugar
finely grated rind of 1 lemon
750 ml full-cream milk
75 g butter
15 ml vanilla essence
4 egg yolks
60 ml smooth apricot or peach jam
MERINGUE
4 egg whites
125 ml castor sugar

Set the oven at 180°C. Lightly butter a 1,5 litre oven-to-table baking dish.

Mix the crumbs, castor sugar and lemon rind in a bowl. Heat the milk to boiling point in a medium saucepan. Remove from the heat, stir in the butter and vanilla essence and pour into the crumb mixture. Set aside for 10 minutes for the crumbs to absorb the milk, then beat in the egg yolks. (Do this very well so that the pudding bakes evenly.)

Pour into the buttered baking dish and bake, uncovered, for 45 minutes. Warm the jam, then spoon it carefully over the surface as evenly as possible.

MERINGUE Beat the egg white stiffly, then gradually beat in the castor sugar. Spread onto the pudding, making pretty peaks. Return it to the oven for 10 minutes until meringue-tips are golden. Serve warm.

SERVES 8

SAGO PUDDING
WITH VAN DER HUM SAUCE

Early recipes sweetened this English pudding with honey, and added naartjie (tangerine) peel for extra flavour. Rose water may be used in place of vanilla essence. Cape Malays add favourite spices such as cinnamon and cardamom. The sauce is optional.

200 ml sago
750 ml full-cream milk
80 ml sugar
finely grated rind of 1 small lemon
1 ml salt
1 ml grated nutmeg
50 g butter
125 ml cream
15 ml vanilla essence
3 eggs
grated nutmeg or ground cinnamon
VAN DER HUM SAUCE
4 oranges
15 ml cornflour
60 ml sugar
30 ml Van der Hum (or another citrus-based liqueur)

Set the oven at 160°C. Butter a 2 litre oven-to-table baking dish. Combine the sago, milk, sugar, lemon rind, salt and nutmeg in a medium saucepan. Bring to the boil, stirring continuously, then remove from the heat, cover and set aside for 15 minutes for the sago to plump. Stir occasionally.

Beat in the butter, cream, vanilla essence and eggs. Pour into the baking dish, and sprinkle a little nutmeg or cinnamon on top. Place in a larger baking dish, add boiling water to come halfway up the sides, and bake uncovered for about 45 minutes until set. Serve warm.

SAUCE Finely grate the rind of one orange. Peel and cut out the segments of all four oranges. Squeeze the remaining juice into a measuring jug. You should have 250 ml (if necessary make up with extra juice). Mix in the cornflour and rind, pour into a small saucepan with the sugar and bring to the boil, stirring until the sugar dissolves and the sauce is clear. Cool, then add the orange segments and Van der Hum.

SERVES 8

BREAD AND BUTTER PUDDING

This comfort-zone favourite is as popular here as it is in England, where the recipe originated. It is best made with bread that is past its prime. Some cooks cut off the crusts; others leave them on for added texture. One may add goodies like toasted almonds and candied orange rind, but there really is no need, though a splash of brandy or sherry perks things up, and a touch of spice – a few cardamom pods – adds a Cape-Malay flavour.

8 slices white bread
butter, smooth apricot jam, sultanas
500 ml milk
1 stick cinnamon
grated rind of 1 small lemon
60 ml sugar
10 ml vanilla essence
3 eggs
30 ml brandy or medium sherry
(optional)
sugar
grated nutmeg or ground cinnamon

Butter a large oven-to-table dish. Butter the bread liberally and spread with jam. Cut into triangles and lay in the baking dish, slices overlapping a little. Scatter sultanas between the slices, not on top. (If they rise to the surface of the pud they may burn.)

Scald the milk with the cinnamon and lemon rind. Set aside for 15 minutes for flavours to infuse. Discard cinnamon then beat in the sugar, vanilla essence, eggs and brandy or sherry. Pour carefully into the dish (don't swish off the jam), and set aside for about 1 hour to allow the liquid to soak in.

Meanwhile set the oven at 160°C. Place the pudding in a larger baking dish, add boiling water to come halfway up the sides and bake uncovered for 45 minutes. Sprinkle sugar, and a little nutmeg or cinnamon on the surface about 10 minutes before the end of the cooking time, and increase the oven temperature to glaze the pudding.

SERVES 6

BOEBER

*There are probably as many recipes for boeber as
there are Cape Malay cooks! Some spell it 'boeboer',
others 'bubur'; some reduce the amount of sago, and offer it
as a warm, spicy milk drink; others offer it as a warm pudding.
Some add milk, others prefer condensed milk.
Everyone serves it after sunset on the 15th day of Ramadan
to celebrate the middle of the fast. A similar Indian milk
pudding, called doodh pak, is made either with
vermicelli or basmati rice.*

45 ml sago
1 litre milk
100 g flaked almonds
80 g butter
200 ml vermicelli
5 cardamom pods, cracked
1 stick cinnamon
80 ml sugar
125 ml sultanas
250 ml cream or condensed milk
30 ml rose water
ground cinnamon

Place the sago in a small saucepan with 250 ml of the milk.
Bring to the boil, stirring continuously. Remove from the
heat, cover and set aside for 15 minutes to plump.

Toast the almonds in a dry frying pan until golden and
aromatic. Allow to cool.

Melt the butter in a medium saucepan. Add the vermicelli, cardamom and cinnamon and stir over very low heat
until golden and aromatic.

Add the remaining milk, sugar, sultanas and sago (with
the milk), and cook over low heat for about 15 minutes until
vermicelli is tender and sago is transparent. Stir occasionally at first, then constantly as the boeber thickens.

Remove from the heat and stir in the almonds, cream or
condensed milk, and rose water. Spoon into a pudding bowl,
sprinkle with cinnamon and serve warm. Although boeber is
extremely rich, you're welcome to offer it with lightly
whipped cream.

SERVES 6-8

CAPE BRANDY PUDDING

*Rich, light, syrupy, supremely satisfying, and
named after brandy (fire water), which has been
distilled in the country since 1672. Malva Pudding and
Cape Brandy Pudding are always presented as
part of the dessert line-up at country-style buffets,
and many visitors to South Africa say they are a
culinary highlight of their trip.*

250 g pitted dates, roughly
chopped
250 ml water
5 ml bicarbonate of soda
100 g soft butter
200 ml castor sugar
1 egg
250 ml flour
5 ml baking powder
1 ml salt
100 g pecan nuts or walnuts,
roughly crumbled
SYRUP
125 ml sugar
60 ml water
60 ml brandy
5 ml vanilla essence
15 ml butter

Set the oven at 180°C. Butter a baking dish. Combine the
dates and water in a small saucepan and bring to the boil,
mixing lightly. Remove from heat, stir in bicarb and cool.

Cream together the butter, sugar and egg. Sift in the flour,
baking powder and salt and mix lightly. Stir in the date mixture and fold in the nuts. Pour into the baking dish and
bake, uncovered, for 45 minutes.

SYRUP Combine the sugar and water in a saucepan, and
bring to the boil, stirring to dissolve the sugar. Remove from
the heat and mix in the brandy, vanilla essence and butter.

Pour over the warm pudding as it comes out of the oven
and offer whipped cream separately if you wish. This pudding reheats perfectly. Cover and chill for up to a day.

SERVES 8

MALVA PUDDING

Marshmallow pudding –
named for its spongy texture –
is a favourite Cape Dutch winter recipe.

250 ml sugar
1 egg
15 ml soft butter
60 ml smooth apricot jam
250 ml cake flour
5 ml bicarbonate of soda
1 ml salt
250 ml milk
10 ml vinegar
10 ml vanilla essence

250 ml cream or evaporated milk
100 g unsalted butter
125 ml sugar
60 ml hot water

Set the oven at 180°C. Beat together the sugar, egg, butter and jam until pale and fluffy. Sift together the flour, bicarb and salt. Mix together the milk, vinegar and vanilla essence. Fold alternately into the egg mixture until thoroughly mixed. Pour into a buttered baking dish, cover with lightly oiled foil and bake for about 45 minutes until firm.

While the pudding is baking combine the remaining ingredients in a saucepan. Heat, stirring, until the butter melts and the sugar has dissolved. Pour over the hot pudding. Serve warm with softly whipped cream.

SERVES 6

CHAPTER SEVENTEEN
BREADS
& HOMEBAKES

A STORY THAT DID the rounds in the 1890s claimed that the merits of 'delicately nurtured' girls visiting their brothers in the African wilds (presumably to add a feminine touch to the rough life of far-flung outposts of the Empire) were judged entirely on their bread-making skills.

The same is true of all South Africans, who delight in offering bread and other home-baked goodies to family and friends.

Breads reflect the varied predilections of our diverse communities – the dumplings of rural blacks, Malay roti, hearty Cape-Dutch wholewheat loaves, and Indian baked, fried, griddle-cooked and tandoori breads among them.

LEFT *Tea-time at Carrigans Country Estate in Mpumalanga. Chocolate Cake with Date and Nut Filling (page 214), Soetkoekies (page 207).*
ABOVE *Herbed Beer Bread (page 204), with a selection of cheeses.*

For early wandering pastoralists and trek-farmers, hollowed out ant heaps made perfect bakoonde (baking ovens). Voortrekkers pressed their trusty three-legged potjies into service as a baking receptacle. Clay ovens – some large enough to accommodate forty loaves at one go – came later. A fire was lit inside the door, then pushed to the back of the oven and more fuel added. After about an hour of fire-tending, the oven was hot enough. Fire and ash were raked out and bread pans of risen dough were deposited inside, using long-handled broodskoppe (bread planks). The door was closed and sealed with clay.

Tribal black folk baked in mud ovens – a hole in the ground with shelves to hold the cakes and breads. Alternatively, maize, sorghum and millet-meal dumplings were steamed on sticks criss-crossed in a water-filled clay pot.

When communities became more settled, outside brick ovens were built, then contraptions were modernised and brought indoors to the kitchen – the heart of every home.

Early breads were made from flour crushed between stones powered by perdemeule (horse mills). Though unleavened, trace elements from the grinding stones added to the raising ability of the flour.

Various pre-yeast raising agents included sourdough yeast made from hops and potatoes, and crushed raisins mixed with sugar and tepid water. Palm wine stirred into salt and sugar was the standard raising agent of West Coast bread, and Karoo bakers used the root of a rare plant, which was considered superior even to yeast and baking powder.

Cake-baking came into its own after Britain usurped Holland as rulers of the Cape in the early 1800s. Rather than reflect any intrinsic South African character, however, cakes and tarts echoed fashionable European trends of the time.

The best way to judge our enthusiasm for sweet things and our skills in baking is to attend a fête, festival or family celebration of any sort. The array of delicious goodies decorated with glacé fruit, silver dragees, whipped cream, nuts and coconut speaks for itself – and of folk who take pleasure is baking up a storm at every opportunity.

 Melktert (page 212) with Hertzog Cookies (behind left, page 208) and Buttermilk Rusks (page 208).

PURI

A Cape Malay speciality; deep fried puffs of dough, which are offered with curry instead of rice. They are also delicious with a bowl of soup.

250 ml cake flour
2 ml salt
30 ml vegetable oil
100 ml water (approximate amount)

Sift the flour and salt into a bowl. Mix together the oil and water and blend in to make a soft dough. Knead on a floured surface until smooth and elastic.

Break off small pieces and roll out thinly into circles. Deep fry in hot oil until puffed, crisp and golden – hold the puri under the oil if they rise to the surface. Drain on kitchen paper and serve warm.

MAKES ABOUT 12

MAIZE BREAD

Maize makes delicious bread, whether the meal or corn kernels are used. Recipes both traditional and modern (like this one) are prepared by cooks across the social spectrum.

500 ml cake flour
10 ml baking powder
5 ml salt
125 ml maize meal
340 g can whole kernel corn, drained
3 eggs
175 ml plain yoghurt

Set the oven at 200°C. Grease a small loaf tin. Sift the flour, baking powder and salt into a bowl. Mix in the maize meal and corn kernels. Beat together the eggs and yoghurt, mix in, and pour into the tin. Bake for 1¼ hours until a skewer comes out clean. Turn out onto a wire rack to cool. Delicious with butter and grated cheese.

MAKES 1 SMALL LOAF

ROTI

Pancake-like roti are designed so that curry-lovers can tear off pieces and scoop up the meat and gravy in one go. Salomi – roti rolled around a spoonful of curried mince – is a unique Cape-Malay fast-food take-out, popular as a snack or light lunch.

750 ml cake flour
5 ml salt
45 ml vegetable oil
300 ml water (approximate amount)
80 g very soft butter

Sift the flour and salt into a large bowl. Add the oil and rub in with your fingertips until the mixture is crumbly. Add sufficient water to make a fairly soft dough. Turn out onto a floured surface and roll out to the size of a baking tray. Spread with soft butter and roll up. Cover with a tea towel and allow to rest for at least 30 minutes.

Cut off pieces and roll into balls between your palms. Roll out on a floured surface; stack, interleaved with waxed paper.

Fry in hot oil until pale golden on each side. Drain on kitchen paper and serve warm.

MAKES ABOUT 12

FARMHOUSE SEED BREAD

The cultivation of grains like wheat, rye, barley, oats, buckwheat and maize was slow to develop at the Cape, and supplies had to be brought by ship from the East. But after free burghers were encouraged to plant cereal crops, grain production improved no end. This luxurious, healthy loaf is crammed with seeds; use whichever you prefer – or omit them entirely and increase the amount of wholewheat flour accordingly.

500 g (1 litre) wholewheat flour
250 ml self-raising flour
250 ml molasses bran
60 ml sunflower seeds
60 ml sesame seeds
60 ml poppy seeds
60 ml linseeds
60 ml brown sugar
15 ml salt
30 ml vegetable oil
20 g (2 sachets) instant dried yeast
1 litre tepid water (approximate amount)
extra nuts

Oil one large or two small loaf tins – round or oblong, as you prefer. Tip the wholewheat flour into a large mixing bowl, sift in the self-raising flour and add the bran, seeds, brown sugar, salt, oil and yeast. Mix lightly but thoroughly, then add water and mix to a nice dough. (The amount of water required may vary, so don't add it all at once.) When it is the correct consistency, the dough should plop off your hand back into the bowl.

Place the dough into the loaf tin/s and sprinkle extra nuts on top. Cover loosely with oiled plastic wrap and leave in a warm, draught-free spot until double in bulk. Meanwhile set the oven at 180°C. Bake bread for 40 minutes until it sounds hollow when tapped. Turn out on a wire rack to cool.
TO BAKE OVER THE COALS Place dough in a medium potjie well smeared with butter. Place on a grid over the coals and bake, covered, for about 1 hour – test with a skewer. To brown the top, heap medium-cool coals onto the lid during the last 20 minutes or so.

MAKES 1 LARGE OR 2 SMALL LOAVES

HERBED BEER BREAD

750 ml cake flour
5 ml salt
15 ml baking powder
2 ml bicarbonate of soda
30 ml brown sugar
125 ml chopped fresh herbs
340 ml bottle beer
1 egg
2 ml salt

Set the oven to 160°C. Grease a small loaf tin. Sift together the flour, salt, baking powder and bicarb. Lightly mix in the brown sugar and herbs. Pour in the beer and knead lightly to form a stiff dough. Plop the dough into the loaf tin, brush with combined egg and salt, and bake for 60 minutes. Turn out onto a wire rack to cool before serving.

MAKES 1 SMALL LOAF

WHITE BREAD

Long before the world switched to more healthy wholewheat bread, white bread was preferred, and the delicious aroma of baking would emanate from old-fashioned wood-fired ovens and cast-iron pots nestled in the coals. This milk loaf is even more flavourful than plain white bread.

1 kg cake flour
10 ml salt
40 g (4 sachets) instant dried yeast
10 ml sugar
60 g butter, cut into small blocks
600 ml warm milk
1 egg yolk, lightly beaten

Grease two small loaf tins. Sift the flour, salt, yeast and sugar into a bowl. Mix the butter into the warm milk, pour into the dry ingredients and mix to a firm dough. Turn onto a floured surface and knead until smooth and elastic. Place in a lightly oiled bowl, seal with oiled plastic wrap and set aside in a warm spot until double in bulk.

Punch dough down, knead lightly, form into small balls and pack into the loaf tins – they should come about halfway up the side. Place in a warm, draught-free spot for about 30 minutes until the dough reaches the top edge of the tins. Set the oven at 180°C. Brush the dough with egg yolk and bake for 15 minutes. Reduce oven temperature to 160°C and bake for a further 30 minutes until done. Turn out onto a wire rack to cool.

MAKES 2 SMALL LOAVES

KARAMONK SCRAPS

Extra crisp, spicy Malay biscuits flavoured with cardamom.

200 g soft butter
60 ml vegetable oil
250 ml sugar
2 eggs, lightly beaten
500 ml cake flour
5 ml baking powder
1 ml salt
7 ml ground cardamom
5 ml ground cinnamon
15 ml ground Dried Naartjie Peel (page 218)
500 ml desiccated coconut
glacé orange peel or glacé cherries

Herbed Beer Bread (page 204), with olives added to the mix, to complement the accompanying cheeses.

Set the oven at 180°C. Cream together the butter, oil and sugar until pale and fluffy. Beat in the eggs. Sift in the flour, baking powder, salt, cardamom, cinnamon and ground naartjie peel and mix in. Add the coconut and mix to a fairly stiff dough.

Roll out to a thickness of about 5 mm on a floured surface, and cut into rounds with a biscuit cutter. Arrange on lightly greased baking trays and decorate with pieces of glacé orange peel or cherries. Bake for 12-15 minutes until golden. Lift onto wire racks to cool. Store in an airtight container.
MAKES ABOUT 100

VETKOEK

*These simple goodies – literally translated as 'fat cakes' – have
filled many an empty tummy that couldn't wait for bread to bake
in farmhouse kitchens. Bits of dough would be pinched off,
allowed to rise and deep-fried in dripping. Though vetkoek dates
from way back, its appeal has not waned, and modern cookery
books still contain versions of the recipe. In this basic recipe the
mixture is more like a thick batter, which fries up light and crisp.
Serve vetkoek at a braai with a little salt, or break them open
and fill with a savoury filling – this is how they are given as gifts
by Cape Malays during Ramadan. They are also delicious
sprinkled with cinnamon sugar or drizzled with honey, syrup
or jam as a tea-time treat.*

500 ml cake flour
15 ml baking powder
2 ml salt
200 ml milk
1 egg, lightly beaten

Sift together the flour, baking powder and salt into a bowl.
Mix together the milk and egg, and mix in to make a well-
blended, smooth dough. Break off smallish pieces and deep
fry in hot oil until golden and crisp. Drain, and serve warm.
MAKES ABOUT 12

SOETKOEKIES

*These were also called ouma's spice biscuits, as grannies can
always be relied on to find the time to bake sweet treats for
younger members of the family! If you wish to tart up the
presentation, press a piece of flaked almond into
each biscuit before baking.*

200 g soft butter
500 g sugar
500 g cake flour
7 ml baking powder
7 ml bicarbonate of soda
7 ml ground cinnamon
7 ml grated nutmeg
7 ml ground cloves
7 ml ground ginger
1 ml salt
7 ml aniseed
30 ml ground Dried Naartjie Peel (page 218)
1 egg, lightly beaten

Cream together the butter and sugar until pale and fluffy.
Sift together the flour, baking powder, bicarb, cinnamon,
nutmeg, cloves, ginger and salt, and mix in the aniseed and
ground naartjie peel. Mix into creamed mixture with the
beaten egg until blended into a fairly stiff dough.

Grease baking trays. Set the oven at 200°C. Roll out the
dough to a thickness of 5 mm on a floured surface, cut out
rounds with a pastry cutter and arrange on the baking trays.
Alternatively, pinch off pieces the size of walnuts, place on
the trays and press with a fork to flatten slightly. Allow
space between the biscuits, as they will spread slightly as
they cook. Bake for about 15 minutes until golden. Cool on
a wire rack. Store in an airtight container.
MAKES 60-70

Yasmina Stellenboom offers her son, Uzair, traditional Cape-Malay homebakes.

BUTTERMILK RUSKS

750 g (1,5 litres) self-raising flour
5 ml salt
125 ml sugar
200 g soft butter, cut into blocks
500 ml buttermilk
2 eggs, lightly beaten

Grease and flour two small loaf tins. Set the oven at 180°C. Sift together the flour, salt and sugar. Rub in the butter until the mixture is finely crumbled. Mix together the buttermilk and eggs, add and knead to a soft dough.

Roll on a floured surface into a fat sausage and divide into sixteen balls. Pack into the prepared loaf tins; they should come about two-thirds of the way to the rim.

Bake for 30 minutes; reduce oven temperature to 160°C for 30 minutes more. Remove rusks from the tins, break apart, and break each one in half. Arrange on baking trays. Reduce the oven temperature to 100°C and dry the rusks for another 3-4 hours. Cool on a rack. Store in an airtight container.

MAKES 32 RUSKS

HERTZOG COOKIES

These are named after General JBM Hertzog, first prime minister of the Union of South Africa between 1924 and 1939.

Rich Shortcrust Pastry (page 218) made with
self-raising flour
450 g can smooth apricot jam
4 egg whites
250 ml castor sugar
2 ml vanilla essence
500 ml desiccated coconut

Roll out the pastry on a floured surface and cut into rounds. Line greased patty pans with pastry and fill with apricot jam.

Set the oven at 180°C. Beat the egg white stiffly, then add the castor sugar 60 ml at a time, beating well after each addition. Beat in the vanilla essence. Gently fold in the coconut. Spoon onto the jam in each cookie and bake for about 15 minutes until the topping is golden. Cool for a few minutes in the pans, then lift out and cool on wire racks.

MAKES 24-36, DEPENDING ON SIZE.

CRUMPETS

This recipe for crumpets (or flapjacks, as they are also known) was brought here by our British forebears. A local variation is the addition of buttermilk. They are best served straight from the pan, but the batter may be prepared several hours in advance. They were photographed at the Mount Nelson Hotel.

500 ml cake flour

15 ml baking powder

2 ml salt

45 ml castor sugar

30 ml vegetable oil or melted butter

2 eggs

125 ml buttermilk

250 ml milk

Sift together the flour, baking power, salt and castor sugar. Lightly mix together the oil or melted butter, eggs, buttermilk and milk, and mix in to form a smooth batter.

Heat a little oil in a frying pan, drop in spoonfuls of batter and cook until golden and the surface bubbles pop. Flip over and cook the other side. Drain on kitchen paper.

MAKES ABOUT 36

BRAN MUFFINS WITH RAISINS

The craze for American muffins has reached our shores, and may now be found in many different guises, and offered for breakfast and at tea-time. If you wish to make only half the quantity of muffins, store the remaining, uncooked mixture in the fridge.

125 g soft butter

250 ml sugar

2 eggs, lightly beaten

125 ml bran

650 ml self-raising flour

5 ml ground cinnamon

2 ml salt

400 ml milk

250 ml sultanas

Set the oven at 200°C. Grease muffin tins. Cream together the butter and sugar until pale and fluffy. Mix in the eggs and bran. Sift in the self-raising flour, cinnamon and salt, and fold in with the milk and sultanas. Spoon into the muffin tins. Bake for 20 minutes. Cool on a wire rack.

APPLE MUFFINS Peel 2 Granny Smith apples, slice into slim wedges. Nestle two chips into each uncooked muffin and sprinkle with sugar.

MAKES ABOUT 24

KOEKSISTERS

In the late 1700s the worth of many a wife was measured by the quality of her koeksisters – syrupy Batavian delectations which are among our most popular (and fattening!) traditional treats. One enthusiastic koeksister-maker was affectionately nicknamed Betje Bolletjie in deference to her extraordinary skills in this department, and she sold her wares far and wide. The odd name is believed to have come from two eccentric Dutch sisters who first had the notion to plait their doughnuts, little knowing they would be immortalized. The secret of success is in the the preparation. If possible, make both syrup and dough a day ahead; the syrup should be well chilled and the dough well rested. Deep fry as soon as possible after plaiting, and dip into syrup while still hot. Store lightly covered on a tray – not in an airtight container, or they will lose their crackly crunch.

SYRUP

500 ml water

1 kg sugar

2 ml cream of tartar

2 thin slices ginger, or

2 ml ground ginger

finely grated rind and juice of 1 lemon

DOUGH

500 g (1 litre) cake flour

30 ml baking powder

2 ml salt

50 g butter, cut into small blocks

1 egg

250 ml milk, sour milk or buttermilk

SYRUP Combine the ingredients in a large saucepan and bring to the boil, stirring until the sugar dissolves. Boil without stirring for about 5 minutes to form a light syrup. Strain into a large bowl. Cool, then refrigerate until well chilled. DOUGH Sift together the flour, baking powder and salt. Rub in the butter until the mixture is finely crumbled. Whisk the egg with 200 ml of the milk, add to the flour mixture and knead to make a soft, pliable dough. Add remaining milk only if the dough is too stiff. Form into a ball, wrap in waxed paper and chill for a couple of hours – overnight if at all possible.

Roll out on a floured surface to a thickness of 10 mm. Cut into oblongs 8 cm by 4 cm, and cut each into three strips almost to the top. Plait together and pinch ends tightly to seal. Place on a tray and cover with a damp cloth.

Deep fry a few at a time in hot oil, turning constantly. Watch the heat: koeksisters take 2-3 minutes to cook through and turn deep golden brown. Drain briefly on kitchen paper, then dip while still hot into cold syrup. (If it warms up, place syrup in a larger bowl of cold water with ice blocks.) Drain excess syrup back into the bowl and drain koeksisters on a rack.

MAKES ABOUT 36

KOESISTERS

Spongier, plumper and spicier than koeksisters (spelt with a 'k') – and never plaited – these traditional Sunday morning Cape-Malay treats were hawked by District Six children, to enthusiastic response from passers-by. Another type of koesister was made with cooked potato; this recipe was invented by Mrs Samsodien of Hanover Street, when there was a shortage of flour during the second world war. Ground, dried naartjie peel may be added for extra flavour.

500 g cake flour

100 ml sugar

2 ml salt

10 g (1 sachet) instant dried yeast

10 ml ground ginger

10 ml ground cinnamon

10 ml ground aniseed

5 ml ground cardamom

125 ml vegetable oil

1 egg

200 ml milk

200 ml water

desiccated coconut

SYRUP

500 ml water

250 ml sugar

1 ml bicarbonate of soda

15 ml butter

Sift together the flour, sugar, salt, yeast and spices into a bowl. Lightly mix together the oil and egg, and mix in well.

Mix together the milk and water, heat to blood temperature, and mix in to form a soft dough. Place in an oiled bowl, cover and set aside in a warm spot until double in bulk (about 2 hours, depending on the weather).

Roll out with your hands on a lightly oiled surface into a sausage about 5 cm thick. Cut into 2-cm lengths, form into flattened doughnut shapes and arrange on a tray; leave space for rising. Cover and set aside for about 30 minutes until double in size.

SYRUP Bring the water and sugar to the boil in a large saucepan, stirring until the sugar dissolves. Boil uncovered for about 5 minutes until thickened to a light syrup. Stir in the bicarb and butter.

Deep fry koesisters in medium-hot oil for about 5 minutes, turning constantly, until golden, crisp and cooked through. Drain briefly on kitchen paper. Add to the syrup and simmer gently for about 30 minutes. Lift onto a plate and garnish with a sprinkling of coconut. Koesisters are best eaten within a few hours of being fried.

MAKES ABOUT 30

APPLE TART

*Open pies – a feature of old Cape cookery – were
imitations of the old-fashioned Dutch 'taart',
themselves copies of earlier uncovered pies that
probably came from the East.
Some cooks covered the pie with strips
of pastry to form a lattice, and brushed it
with egg yolk mixed with brandy,
and a little saffron to give a rich, golden colour.*

Rich Shortcrust Pastry (page 218) made
with cake flour
4 Granny Smith apples
30 ml brandy
60 ml sugar
3 whole cloves
30 g (30 ml) butter
30 ml seedless raisins

TOPPING
4-5 small ripe eating apples
60 ml smooth apricot jam
30 ml lemon juice

Set the oven at 200°C. Roll out the pastry on a floured surface and line a shallow 26-cm pie plate. Bake blind.

Peel, core and slice the apples. Place in a saucepan with
the brandy, sugar, cloves, butter and raisins. Cover and cook
very gently, stirring occasionally, for about 15 minutes until
tender. If necessary cook uncovered for a few minutes more
until the liquid has become syrupy. Allow to cool, then
spread the filling into the pastry case.

TOPPING Peel, quarter and core the apples, slice thinly
and arrange on the filling, overlapping the slices. Cover the
tart completely to prevent the glaze from seeping through.
Melt the jam with the lemon juice in a saucepan; spoon
evenly over the apples and bake for 20 minutes.
SERVES 10

MELKTERT

East meets West in this famous Dutch milk tart, which is usually baked in a deep enamel dish, though a quiche tin may be used. In summer, pastry dough was made late at night, wrapped in a damp muslin cloth and hung in a draft to keep cool. For the lightest crust, the tart was baked before sunrise. The custard was flavoured with dried naartjie (tangerine) peel, blanched almonds and peach kernels, and coconut milk or sweet wine were sometimes added. Some modern cooks add a dash of almond essence.

400 g puff pastry or flaky pastry
500 ml full-cream milk
1 stick cinnamon
3 eggs, separated
80 ml cake flour
15 ml cornflour
80 ml castor sugar
2 ml baking powder
30 g (30 ml) butter
15 ml vanilla essence
ground cinnamon

CRUST Set the oven at 200°C. Lightly grease a 24-cm shallow enamel plate or quiche tin. Roll out the pastry and line the baking plate or tin. Press in a piece of oiled foil and bake for 10 minutes. Remove foil and bake the crust for about 5 minutes more until crisp and golden. Allow to cool.

FILLING Measure three-quarters of the milk into a saucepan, add the cinnamon and heat to just below boiling point. Set aside to infuse for about 15 minutes.

Mix together the remaining milk, egg yolks, flour, cornflour, castor sugar and baking powder. Strain in the cinnamon-flavoured milk, pour into a clean saucepan and cook, stirring, until the custard thickens. Remove from the heat, and whisk in the butter and vanilla essence. Cool to room temperature. Reduce oven temperature to 180°C.

Whisk the egg white stiffly and fold into the custard. Pour into the pastry shell and bake for 10 minutes. Reduce oven temperature to 160°C and bake for about 30 minutes more, until the filling is set. Slide the hot tart onto a plate, sprinkle with ground cinnamon and serve warm.

SERVES 8

LEMON MERINGUE PIE

This pie pops up regularly at farm stalls and fêtes. Use full-cream condensed milk and the juice of yellow lemons, otherwise the filling may not set.

Rich Shortcrust Pastry (page 218) made
with cake flour
2 X 397 g cans full-cream condensed milk
4 eggs, separated
200 ml freshly squeezed juice of yellow lemons
30 ml castor sugar

Set the oven at 200°C. Roll out the pastry on a floured surface and line a shallow 22-cm pie plate. Bake blind. Cool.

Mix together the condensed milk, egg yolks and lemon juice, pour into crust and chill for a couple of hours until set.

Just before serving, preheat the oven griller. Whip the egg white until stiff enough to form peaks. Beat in the castor sugar until the mixture is stiff and glossy. Pile onto the tart to form peaks and brown under the griller – watch carefully, the meringue burns in a flash!

SERVES 12

CHOCOLATE CAKE
WITH DATE AND NUT FILLING

500 ml self-raising flour

375 ml castor sugar

2 ml salt

5 ml bicarbonate of soda

60 ml cocoa powder

125 g butter

300 ml milk

5 ml vanilla essence

2 eggs

DATE AND WALNUT FILLING

30 ml cocoa powder

125 ml sugar

125 ml water

15 ml butter

125 g finely chopped pitted dates

15 ml cornflour

30 ml port

50 g finely chopped walnuts or pecan nuts

CHOCOLATE-CREAM ICING

100 g soft butter

200 ml icing sugar, sifted

80 ml cocoa powder, sifted

1 egg, lightly beaten

5 ml vanilla essence

Set the oven at 170°C. Grease and flour a 23-cm cake tin. Sift together the self-raising flour, castor sugar, salt, bicarb and cocoa powder.

Melt the butter and lightly whisk in the milk, vanilla essence and eggs. Mix into the dry ingredients. Pour into the cake tin and bake for 45 minutes until cooked (when a skewer comes out clean). Turn out onto a cake rack to cool.

FILLING Mix together the cocoa powder, sugar, water, butter and dates in a small saucepan. Heat while mashing the dates with a fork. Simmer until thick and smooth, stirring occasionally. Mix together the cornflour and port, add and stir until the mixture thickens. Allow to cool. Stir in the nuts.

ICING Beat all the ingredients together until well blended.

Cut the cake into two layers, sandwich together with filling; cover top and sides with chocolate-cream icing.

214

QUEEN OF SHEBA CAKE

An adaptation of a light, luscious Victorian cake,
which was rediscovered by Letitia Prinsloo, principal of
L'Institut Culinaire in Stellenbosch.
The recipe was brought to South Africa by British settlers.

100 g soft butter
150 ml sugar
3 eggs, separated
200 g dark chocolate, broken into blocks
100 g ground almonds
15 ml cocoa powder
15 ml cake flour
2 ml baking powder
30 ml orange juice
15 ml orange liqueur
5 ml vanilla essence
10 ml finely grated orange rind
1 ml salt
1 ml cream or tartar

Set the oven at 160°C. Grease and line a 20-cm cake tin. Cream together the butter and sugar until pale and fluffy. Add the egg yolks one by one, mixing in well each time.

Soften the chocolate in a bowl over simmering water. Mix until smooth and stir into the egg mixture with the ground almonds. Sift in the cocoa powder, flour and baking powder and fold in with the orange juice, liqueur, vanilla essence and orange rind.

Beat the egg white stiffly with the salt and cream of tarter. Fold into the batter, pour into the cake tin and bake for about 50 minutes until cooked (when a skewer comes out clean). Loosen the edges and place on a rack to cool in the tin. Unmould and serve with berries.
SERVES 10-12

Chocolate Cake with Date and Nut Filling, served with
whipped cream and fresh dates.

215

PANTRY

CHICKEN STOCK

2 litres cold water
1 raw chicken carcass, with trimmings and giblets
(not the liver)
1 onion or 4 leeks, roughly sliced
1 rib celery with leaves, roughly chopped
1-2 carrots, roughly chopped
1 fresh or dried bunch of herbs
(parsley, thyme, bay leaf)
2 ml black peppercorns

Combine all the ingredients in a large saucepan, cover and bring to the boil. Reduce the heat and simmer very gently for 2-3 hours. Strain, pressing on the solids to extract as much of the liquid as possible. Chill or freeze the stock.
MAKES ABOUT 1 LITRE

FISH STOCK

1,5 litres cold water
1 kg rinsed white fish bones, heads and trimmings,
discard bitter gills and entrails
1 onion, quartered
1 carrot, roughly chopped
1 rib celery with leaves, roughly chopped
1 fresh or dried bunch of herbs
(parsley, fennel, bay leaf)
1 strip lemon rind
12 black peppercorns

Combine the ingredients in a large saucepan, cover and bring to the boil. Move the lid aside to partially cover the saucepan and simmer very, very gently for 30 minutes. Strain through a colander lined with several layers of 'kitchen wipes'. Press on the solids to extract as much of the liquid as possible. Chill or freeze the stock.
MAKES ABOUT 1 LITRE

MEAT STOCK

1,5 kg veal, beef, lamb or venison bones
2 onions, quartered
2 carrots, quartered
2-3 ribs celery with leaves, roughly chopped
80 ml vegetable oil
100 g can tomato paste
300 ml dry red wine
2 litres cold water
1 fresh or dried bunch of herbs
(parsley, thyme, bay leaf)

Set the oven at 180°C. Place the bones in a roaster with the onions, carrots and celery. Pour the oil over, mix in lightly and bake, uncovered for about 3 hours until well browned. Turn the ingredients occasionally.

Mix together the tomato paste and wine, and stir in to deglaze the pan. Transfer the ingredients to a large saucepan. Add the water and herbs, cover and simmer gently for 3-4 hours (6-8 hours is even better). Skim the surface and boil uncovered until reduced by two-thirds. Strain into a bowl, pressing on the solids to extract as much of the liquid as possible. Chill or freeze the stock.
MAKES ABOUT 750 ML

GHEE

Clarified butter is the very best for frying, as it may be heated to a very high temperature without burning.
Keep chilled for up to two months.

Place 500 g butter in a deep saucepan and boil gently, uncovered, for 10-15 minutes. It will bubble as the water evaporates, and a layer of scum will rise to the surface. Remove from the heat, scoop off the scum and pour off the clear ghee, leaving behind the layer of salt at the bottom. Cool.
MAKES ABOUT 350 GRAMS

ROASTED MASALA

Like most spices, masalas are available ready-made, but home-made ones are much fresher and more piquantly spiced. If you wish, use roasted masala in place of curry powder.

150 g coriander seeds
125 g cumin seeds
50 g dried red chillies
25 g black peppercorns
2 cinnamon sticks, broken into small pieces
5 g whole cloves
15 ml cardamom pods, lightly crushed
25 g turmeric
25 g ground ginger

Place the coriander, cumin, chillies, peppercorns, cinnamon, cloves and cardamom into a dry frying pan and roast, tossing lightly until the mixture is aromatic. Remove from the heat and mix with the turmeric and ginger. Allow to cool and grind fairly finely with a pestle and mortar or coffee grinder. Store in a screw-topped jar in a cool cupboard, or in the fridge or freezer.
MAKES 400 GRAMS

GARAM MASALA

Always add garam masala at the end of the cooking time, preferably shortly before serving, to retain the fresh flavour.

15 g whole cloves
25 g cumin seeds
25 g coriander seeds
30 g black peppercorns
30 g cardamom pods, lightly crushed
2 cinnamon sticks, broken into small pieces

Roast the ingredients in a dry frying pan to intensify the flavours. Grind fairly finely with a pestle and mortar, or coffee grinder. Store in an airtight container in a cool cupboard, or in the fridge or freezer.
MAKES ABOUT 130 GRAMS

GREEN MASALA

Masala made with fresh chillies (either red or green) is essential in Indian recipes, and may be stored in the fridge for a couple of months.

100 g green chillies, washed and trimmed
50 g green ginger, skin scraped off
30 g garlic cloves, peeled
45 ml vegetable oil
2 ml turmeric
45 ml water

Pound the ingredients into a paste with a pestle and mortar, or in a blender or food processor. Bottle and chill.

GARLIC AND HERB BUTTER

A favourite basting sauce for braaiing or grilling vegetables and all types of seafood – and a simple sauce to serve them with.

200 g butter
juice of 1 lemon
6 cloves garlic, crushed
30 ml chopped fresh herbs (parsley, fennel, thyme)
salt, milled black pepper

Melt the butter in a small saucepan, add the lemon juice, garlic, herbs, and salt and pepper and sizzle for 1 minute.
MAKES ABOUT 250 ML

CRUSHED GARLIC AND CRUSHED GINGER

Crushed garlic and ginger may be packed into screw-topped jars and stored in the fridge for up to a month.

GARLIC Peel the cloves of a couple of heads of garlic, and crush in a food processor with a little vegetable oil.
GINGER Wash and trim a stem of green ginger, peel it if you wish, and crush in a food processor with a little sherry.

MAYONNAISE

For perfect mayonnaise ensure all ingredients
are at room temperature. If you add the oil too quickly,
mayonnaise may separate.

2 whole eggs
2 egg yolks
5 ml dry English mustard
5 ml salt
2 ml white pepper
30 ml wine vinegar
30 ml lemon juice
750 ml vegetable oil

In a food processor or with an electric mixer whisk the
whole eggs, yolks, mustard, salt and pepper until pale and
thick. With the machine running, gradually add the vinegar
and lemon juice, then pour in the oil in a thin stream. Store
in a screw-topped jar in the fridge for up to 3 weeks.
MAKES 1 LITRE

HERBED TOMATO SAUCE

2 onions, very finely chopped
30 ml olive or vegetable oil
4 large, ripe tomatoes, blanched, peeled
and chopped
or 400 g can whole tomatoes, chopped
(don't drain)
2 ml crushed garlic
30 ml chopped fresh thyme, marjoram or oregano
30 ml chopped fresh parsley
1 ml sugar
1 ml paprika

Heat the oil in a frying pan and fry the onion until lightly
browned. Add the remaining ingredients and cook briskly,
uncovered, stirring occasionally, for about 10 minutes until
the sauce thickens slightly. Check the seasoning and adjust
if necessary. Serve hot.
SERVES 6-8

RICH SHORTCRUST PASTRY

This is a delicious, rich pastry for any sweet tart
about 26-cm in diameter. Make double the quantity if you wish,
and store half in the freezer for later use.

500 ml cake flour or self-raising flour, sifted
1 ml salt
60 ml castor sugar
100 g cold butter, cut into small blocks
3 egg yolks
5 ml vanilla essence
60 ml chilled water (approximate amount)

Mix together the flour, salt and castor sugar. Rub in the butter until the mixture is finely crumbled. Mix together the
egg yolks, vanilla essence and chilled water, and mix into
the dry ingredients to make a soft dough. (Add additional
water if necessary.) Wrap in waxed paper and chill in the
fridge for an hour or two.
TO BAKE BLIND Set the oven at 180°C. Roll out the pastry on a floured surface and line baking tin. Press lightly
oiled heavy foil into the pastry and bake for 10 minutes.
Uncover and bake for 5 minutes more to crisp slightly.
Allow to cool before adding the filling.

DRIED NAARTJIE PEEL

No well-stocked eighteenth- or nineteenth-century
Cape kitchen was without a jar of dried naartjie
(tangerine) peel, which was used to flavour all kinds
of dishes from pastries and cakes to vegetables like
sweet potato and pumpkin. Furthermore, when a piece
was added to a cup of tea, it infused the brew with
a gentle citrus flavour.

Remove the peel in strips from several naartjies and place
on a baking tray. Dry for about 1½ hours until crisp in an
oven preheated to 100°C. Store in an airtight jar until
required. Use the strips or crush them first – with a pestle
and mortar – as required in the recipe. Orange peel may be
dried in the same way.

CINNAMON SUGAR

The flavour of cinnamon is synonymous with Cape cooking and, mixed with sugar, can be sprinkled over anything from puddings to cakes.

Mix about 125 ml sugar with 10 ml cinnamon. Store in a small bottle.

BERRY COULIS

400 g strawberries or raspberries
125 ml castor sugar
2 ml ground cinnamon
lemon juice

Purée the berries with the castor sugar, cinnamon and lemon juice to taste. Strain and discard the pips.

METRIC CONVERSION CHART

In this book, metric measurements have been given. Conversion to standard U.S. and imperial measures are given below, but please remember that the equivalents are not exact, as measurements have been rounded out. Use either metric or imperial measurements, but not a mixture of both.

VOLUME AND LIQUID MEASURES

1 litre	4 cups
750 ml	3 cups
500 ml	2 cups
375 ml	1½ cups
300 ml	1¼ cups
250 ml	1 cup
200 ml	¾ cup
150 ml	⅔ cup
125 ml	½ cup
80 ml	⅓ cup
60 ml	¼ cup
45 ml	3 tablespoons
30 ml	2 tablespoons
20 ml	4 teaspoons
15 ml	1 tablespoon
10 ml	2 teaspoons
7 ml	1½ teaspoons
5 ml	1 teaspoon
2 ml	½ teaspoon
1 ml	¼ teaspoon

WEIGHTS

900 grams	2 lbs
450 grams	1 lb
270 grams	9 oz
230 grams	8 oz
200 grams	7 oz
180 grams	6 oz
140 grams	5 oz
115 grams	4 oz
90 grams	3 oz
60 grams	2 oz
30 grams	½ oz

OVEN TEMPERATURES

Deg C	Deg F	Gas
100	200	1
120	250	1
140	275	2
160	325	2
180	350	3
200	400	4
220	450	5-6

INDEX OF FOODS, CROPS & DISHES

PHOTOGRAPHIC LOCATIONS

CAPE PENINSULA & BOLAND

Alphen Hotel, Constantia

Boschendal Estate, Groot Drakenstein

Cape Manna Restaurant, Cape Town

The Cellars-Hohenort Hotel, Constantia

Claridge Wine Estate, Wellington

Constantia Uitsig, Constantia

D'Ouwe Werf Herberg, Stellenbosch

Grande Roche Hotel, Paarl

Lanzerac Hotel, Stellenbosch

Le Quartier Français, Franschhoek

Leinster Hall Restaurant, Gardens, Cape Town

L'Institut Culinaire, Stellenbosch

Mount Nelson Hotel, Gardens, Cape Town

WEST COAST & NAMAQUALAND

Bushman's Kloof Private Game Reserve, near Clanwilliam

Kuiperskraal Farm, near Durbanville

Marine Protea Hotel, Lambert's Bay

Saldanha Bay Protea Hotel, Saldanha

Strandkombuis, Yzerfontein

Voëlvlei Farm, Piketberg

OVERBERG, GARDEN ROUTE & EASTERN CAPE

The Arniston Hotel, Waenhuiskrans

The Beach House on Sandown Bay, Kleinmond

The Cock House, Grahamstown

Hunters Country House, Plettenberg Bay

The Knysna Oyster Company, Knysna

The Plettenberg, Plettenberg Bay

Shamwari Game Reserve, near Port Elizabeth

Summerhill Farm, Bathurst

KAROO & NORTHERN CAPE

Dennehof Karoo Guest House, Prince Albert

Die Hantamhuise, Calvinia

The Drostdy Hotel, Graaff-Reinet

Groenfontein Farm, Koue Bokkeveld

Kagga Kamma, Koue Bokkeveld

Le Must Restaurant, Upington

Safari Ostrich Show Farm, Oudtshoorn

KWAZULU-NATAL

Eastern Rendezvous, Blue Lagoon, Durban

Joe's Corner Shop, Victoria Street Market, Durban

Old Halliwell Country Inn, Curry's Post, near Howick

Phinda Private Game Reserve

The Royal, Durban

Shakaland, near Eshowe

Shortens Country House, Umhlali

FREE STATE

The Artists' Colony, Smithfield

Bainsvlei Farmers' Market, Bloemfontein

De Oude Kraal Country Lodge, near Bloemfontein

Onze Rust Restaurant, near Bloemfontein

GAUTENG, MPUMALANGA & NORTHERN REGIONS

The Artists' Cafe, Hendriksdal

Carrigans Country Estate, Kiepersol

The Coach House, Agatha, near Tzaneen

Critchley Hackle Lodge, Dullstroom

Cybele Forest Lodge, White River

Glenshiel Country Lodge, Magoebaskloof

KwaNdebele Traditional Village, Gauteng

Lesedi Cultural Village, near Broederstroom

Londolozi Game Reserve, Sabi Sand Game Reserve

Makalali Private Game Reserve, North-East
      Mpumalanga Lowveld

Milly's Trout Farm, near Dullstroom

Old Joe's Kaia, Schoemanskloof

The Palace at The Lost City, Sun City

Sapekoe Tea Estate, Tzaneen

Singita Private Game Reserve, Sabi Sand Game Reserve

Walkersons Country Manor, Dullstroom

Westfalia Estates, near Duiwelskloof

RECIPE INDEX